Praise for *The Book on Mind Management*

"Dr. Deaton's book is one that I will recommend to all my friends and business associates. The techniques he describes *really* work! I currently manage an extremely productive department in a large corporation; however, I am convinced that the productivity would be even greater if everyone in the department read this book and used the techniques. I wish I would have known about and practiced dominant thought management earlier. What a difference it has now made in my life!"

- **Joan Gustafson,** Manager, Productivity and Quality, 3M

"God bless Dennis Deaton! For he is doing the Lord's work, as is so clearly seen in his latest publication *The Book on Mind Management!* WOW! Finally Napoleon Hill meets the 21st century so that we all can put these timeless principles of TRUTH and PERSONAL POWER to work in our lives."

- **Bernhard Dohrmann,** Pres., Income Builders Internat'l
Author: *Living Life as a Super Achiever* and *Money Magic*

"What Dennis is saying is definitely right on, and I believe it is the first step to consciousness in business, as THE MENTAL ATHLETE is the first step to consciousness in sports. Both of them get the person to look at his/her own personal accountability, letting go of blame, and how our minds create our reality. These realizations are of prime importance in building a better, kinder and more humane world."

- **Kay Porter**, Ph.D.; Author: *The Mental Athlete*

The Book on Mind Management is based on Dennis Deaton's Life Management Seminars. Here's what people are saying:

"It is not often that recommended training meets with unanimous positive feedback from its participants, or that I am thanked by them for offering such training. Both experiences have been my pleasure since 'Mind Management' became part of our basic training."

John A. Walters, Analytical Laboratory Manager, TRW

"I just wanted to let you know how effective Dennis Deaton's seminar presentation skills are! Due to applying the Visioneering goal setting techniques, Dennis presented, one of our sales teams ended last year at 118%. They attribute this directly to his seminar."

Sally Eckstein, Branch Manager, AT&T

"Thank you for the excellent products and superior services that you provide. Your courses receive our highest participant ratings. Universally, from management to front line workers, everyone values your seminars. We have achieved success by your dedication to quality and customer service."

Ray Waddoups, Vice President, Motorola University West

"I just wanted to let you know how much we enjoyed the seminar. We were very anxious to bring the information back to Texas Instruments, and are excited about returning to Phoenix to attend other sessions of your program."

Carolyn Odom, TQC/Training, Texas Instruments

"I was inspired by the motivational messages contained in your presentation. But I was delighted with the response of my staff; they were all fired up and set to go out and accomplish great things! I would certainly recommend your training!"

Kalena Graffam, Staffing Manager, VLSI Technology

"Again, let me applaud the outstanding seminar you provided our people this past Monday. In retrospect, I can remember very few seminars where the speaker received a standing ovation at the end."

Carl B. Munro, Director Quality Management, DUPONT

"Dr. Deaton's presentation is such a powerful message for today's corporate community. By the time I got back to my office after the seminar, my mailbox was full of messages saying thanks for bringing Mind Management and Dr. Deaton to AT&T."

Maryanne Shea, Customer Support Manager, AT&T

Also by Dennis R. Deaton

Money: An Owner's Manual

And, live seminars and recorded presentations:

"Life Management"

"Time Management: The Myths and the Mastery"

"Visioneering™: The Art of Power Goaling"

"Money: An Owner's Manual"

"Winning The Inner Game of Life" (Total Mind-Body Fitness)

THE BOOK ON
MIND
MANAGEMENT

by Dennis R. Deaton

MMI Publishing
Mesa, AZ

The Book on Mind Management

By Dennis R. Deaton

Editor:	Cecily Markland
Typesetting:	Tracy Grace
Cover Design:	Robert Allison/Vista Design
Proofreaders:	April Deaton, Susan Deaton, Kerri Markland

Printed in the United States of America

Library of Congress Card Number 94-077280
ISBN 1-881840-34-4 (pbk)
        1-881840-35-2 (hc)

TimeMax, Inc.
1818 E. Southern Avenue
Mesa, AZ 85204
(602) 545-8311

Acknowledgments

I wish to thank those who I cannot thank enough:

Cecily J. Markland, more of a collaborator and colleague than an editor. On several occasions the inspiration she received was patently obvious. Furthermore, her abiding commitment to the book sustained the entire effort throughout.

Reece A. Bawden, a consummate leader, whose commitment to our mutual goals has constituted the differential element of our success.

Stephen D. Chandler, a champion of optimism and hope, for his insights, critiques and solid wisdom on the subject and tenor of the book.

Susan, my able partner in life and beyond, my gift from God.

Finally and emphatically, **The Lord, Jesus Christ**, whose gifts and endowments are impossible to enumerate, let alone begin to repay. Many times throughout this project I have personally experienced the essence of Paul's tribute to the ultimate source of power, "all things are possible through Christ who strengtheneth me." Without His enabling power the entire subject we have undertaken would not only be meaningless, but impossible.

Contents

Power Principles

Index

Foreword

There was a time when I didn't know who Dennis Deaton was.

It is surprising that I didn't, because I was an avid purchaser of all Nightingale-Conant's motivational tapes, and Deaton's own "Visioneering™" series was in that catalogue.

But when the sales manager of a top-rated radio station in the Phoenix market recommended him to me, the name, "Dennis Deaton," did not ring a bell.

But the man has rung many bells since then. Even in that one event—when I invited him to speak at a sales meeting I was conducting for a major car dealer—he rang bells that have not stopped tolling.

The car dealer was a client of mine. I was doing their advertising, and they were having a slow month. The advertisements were drawing traffic, but somehow the sales weren't happening. Could I please find a good speaker who could motivate the troops in a crucial mid-month sales meeting?

I knew of no one in Arizona who was great at public speaking. I had my favorites on the national scene—Anthony Robbins, Wayne Dyer and Tom Peters—but I didn't think anyone local could equal their level of motivational power.

I asked my friend at the radio station if there was anyone in Arizona in that national category, and he said, "Just one."

"I don't know if you can get him for the date you want," said, "but if you can, get him. His name is Dennis Deaton, and he's the best."

Dr. Deaton was out of town speaking when I tracked him down, but he agreed to fly back to Arizona in time for our sales meeting.

He spoke for less than an hour, and the sales people in that room were mesmerized. But even more significantly, they then went out and had the best sales month in their company's history.

Was it purely emotional?

There was emotion, to be sure, in the great stories Dennis told to illustrate his teaching, but in the end—it was the teaching.

What he teaches, changes lives; and it changes lives *quickly*.

My life was so changed by that speech that I made a secret vow on the spot that someday I would go to work for the man I'd just heard.

Two years later I got that chance, and it has been the greatest adventure of my life.

The power in the teaching I heard that day is now in a book, and it is this book that you are holding in your hands.

What happened to those car sales people, and what happened to me, can now happen to you.

The Book on Mind Management is not just a theory. It is not a collection of hypothetical ideas. It is a long-awaited written account of *what works*.

Dennis Deaton has taught this book—in seminar form—to tens of thousands of people all over the world. Fortune 500 companies continue to increase their enrollment in his courses, and sales staffs continue to increase their performance after applying his principles of mind management.

I recommend you read *The Book on Mind Management* at least twice. Read it first for the pure drama of it—relish the inspiring stories and savor the intellectually satisfying explanations of how your mind really works.

But then read it again for power. Read it the second time with your yellow highlighter handy. And once you've highlighted the passages that speak to you, read them aloud.

A lifetime of work is in this book. The man who wrote it will change your life. He changed mine.

By Steve Chandler

SECTION I

THE CAUSE

Until you know causes, you cannot control effects.

IT ALL BEGINS IN THE MIND.

CHAPTER 1

Discovering the Inner Game

Human behavior is an effect: Human thought is the cause. Whatever you do, you do first in your mind. Your mind, the ultimate source of all your actions and reactions, orchestrates every deed, performs every act, authors every word.

THE CONSUMMATE TRUTH OF LIFE

We think, and with those thoughts, we *create*. We create the world we live in. It goes beyond influencing, shaping or guiding. You and I, in very literal terms, determine what we experience and what we enact into the world. We establish our own happiness or misery, abundance or scarcity, bondage or freedom. We harvest in life, only and exactly, what we sow in our minds.

At this very instant, you are abiding the consequences of your own mental choices. You have been where your thoughts have led you, you now stand where your thoughts have brought you, and you will go as high and as far as your thoughts will take you.

All that you do and all that you ever will accomplish is a product of your mind. Once you see (really see) that thought is the sole cause of all your effects, and discover that you have total control over that exclusive causative force, you gain access to the grand key—the source and the solution to the full gamut of human potential.

**The consummate truth of life is that
we alter our destiny by altering our thoughts.
The mind is our most crucial resource, our crowning asset,
our ultimate arena of battle.
If we will master the power of our minds,
we may do or be whatsoever we will.**

I first saw the reality of this when I was a boy. Totally enthralled with baseball, I was one of those devoted fanatics who spent every penny of allowance on baseball cards and slept with his mitt. I loved the game, and I wanted to play it. My desire was huge, but my body wasn't. I was a shrimp.

I am now six-feet tall, but I got my growth very late. Even as a junior in high school, I was only 4'8" and weighed 88 pounds. My first year of organized baseball, playing in a league for boys 9 through 12, I was the smallest kid in the league.

This particular league required no tryouts. Every boy who joined was placed on a team, which was a good thing for me. None of the teams would have beaten down my door to sign me. At the first workout session with my new team, it was clear that my teammates did not consider me an asset. I was deemed a liability. (A kid that small *had* to be an automatic out.)

So new to the territory, and inexperienced as I was in sports, in group psychology and in mind management, I was overwhelmed. I went through the whole season without a hit. (Every team we faced seemed to have a fireball pitcher—a giant, tobacco-chewing, 12-year-old who'd been on steroids for three years.)

My teammates weren't at all disappointed when our family moved away before the next season.

Somehow, and to this day I do not know exactly why, I knew that my performance that season was not a true reflection of my real capability. Deep down I felt I was better than what had shown up on the field. I even sensed that *I was letting* the less-than-generous attitudes of my teammates, and some of their parents, come true. I was fulfilling *their* expectations, not mine. I began to be aware that I was playing two games. There was the outer game of baseball and the inner game of life.

ANOTHER CHANCE

When the next summer rolled around, our family was living in another city. Baseball was still my love and my passion despite my dismal rookie year, and I went out for another team. This league required tryouts, and I got myself prepared. I worked hard on my outer game. I concentrated on building up my arm so I could throw accurately, if not hard. I also gave a great deal of thought to the inner game as well.

I was new. I did not have any friends yet. Nobody knew my past. There were no expectations to live up to, and I realized I was in a rather unique position. Contrary to the adage, I actually *did* have a second chance to make a first impression. Real resolution set in; I was determined to go to those tryouts and, despite my size, show this new town that Dennis Deaton could play baseball.

I not only made a team, it was a good one—one of the contenders for the league championship. That milestone verified something deep inside me. I realized that my brighter prospects were not so much due to any great physical changes; I was still a shrimp. But it was becoming quite clear that I was on this team and gaining respect day by day with my peers because (CLICK) I was playing the inner game so much better.

There had been some remarks at tryouts and at early practices about my size, but I was ready this time. I refused to listen to those comments. I heard them, but I did not listen. I played *my game* this time, not theirs.

By the second game of the season I was starting at second base and played solid defense throughout the season. As the season proceeded, I got a few hits and quite a few walks. (I actually found that being small could be exploited a bit, to the advantage of myself and my team.) I was living my dream, and my appetite for baseball was insatiable. First shoe boxes, and then whole closets, overflowed with cards and stale squares of bubble gum.

Near the end of the season, we were tied for first place in our division. With a win in our final game, we could secure a place in the "championship series" against the powerhouse of our league, the runaway leader in the other division, the dreaded Indians. All we had to do was win the last league game of the season. The problem was, the team we had to beat was The Dreaded Indians.

What made the Indians so feared was their fireball pitcher, Troy Scott. Troy threw bullets. When he pitched, the ball looked more like an aspirin than a baseball when it flew by. I hadn't gotten a hit off him all year long.

The day and night before the game, I could not think of anything but Troy Scott and his wicked fastballs. I wrestled with fear, tussled with doubt, grappled with worry. The pressure mounted in my mind. At times I even wished I wouldn't have to play. I wanted to win in the worst way, but what I had to go through to obtain the win seemed too hard and frightening. I fantasized that perhaps I could just get sick that night, and my teammates would win without me.

When I dwelt on that thought, I realized how stupid I was being. If we won the game we would merely entitle ourselves to play the Indians again. The championship came down to a two-out-of-three games series with the Indians, who had already cinched their division. Why did I even want to win this game, if I feared playing the Indians so much? Winning this game would only result in facing the agony at least two more times after that.

The ridiculousness of my fears began to show up. I realized that I was falling back into the errors of my rookie year. I was losing the inner game. Fear was winning. Yet, somehow, even at the age of 10 years old, I perceived that fear could only win if I allowed that to happen. I sensed that I could overcome if I really chose to, and I began to at least put up some resistance to my mental opponents.

The one element in our favor in this final game was the fact that we were home team and would have last at-bats. As fate or destiny would dictate, it all came down to that last opportunity. The Indians were ahead 2-0, and Troy Scott was showing no sign of compassion or weakness.

I do not recall all the details of how it happened, but we loaded the bases and with one out, I was standing in the on deck circle, praying that my teammate in front of me would deliver the three runners on base. I would then get to celebrate victory with my team without having to face Troy Scott again.

I still remember to this day that my knees were literally trembling as I stood there, hoping I wouldn't have to get into the batter's box again. My fears were not totally unjustified. I had struck out once and walked once, but what was so vivid in my mind was my last at bat. Troy Scott had a fastball get away from him and it had hit me, creating a throbbing bulge on my left thigh.

"Strike three!" the umpire bellowed, as my teammate went down on strikes. My nightmare had been realized. I not only had to get into the batter's box one more time against Troy Scott, the whole game and my team's championship hopes sat squarely on my shrimpy shoulders.

Like most good pitchers, Troy Scott knew something about the inner game too. Intimidation can be a potent tool, and he realized he had it all going for him. He was twice my size, two years older and had already hit me once. He sort of sneered at me as I stepped into the box, I thought, much like a tiger must gloat as it's about to devour a fawn.

The first pitch was purposely inside, and it sent me diving into the dust, fearing instant and excruciating death. I remember getting up and dusting myself off and then stepping back from the plate a few paces. My mind was racing and several things fell into place in rapid succession. I sensed the intimidation— that I was being taken for granted or disrespected or something akin to all that. Emotion started to boil inside. Things still lingering from my rookie season, the bad taste of letting other people "buffalo" me, surged to the surface.

Right then and there, I took charge in the inner game. I gritted my teeth, and I resolved deeply and totally that fear and intimidation and Troy Scott were not going to take me so easily. I stepped into the box again and decided that I was going to stand in there and take a real crack at one of those fastballs. I had achieved, at that moment, a victory in the inner game.

I took a rip at the very next pitch and fouled it off to the right. "Late," I said to myself, "swing faster." On the next pitch or the one after it, I did swing faster, and my bat connected with that Troy Scott fastball, and the ball shot off my bat. It sailed into right center field into the gap, and I was running at full throttle toward first. With two outs, my teammates on base had been running; and they all scored, while I wound up at second base with a double.

CONTEMPLATING THE CAUSE

I have had many happy moments in my life, but none any happier or more exhilarating than that one. I was soaring in a state of bliss. My teammates carried me off the field. I felt like the weight of the entire continent had been lifted from my spine. And during all the celebration and all the euphoria, I was keenly aware of what had precipitated all this. Success in the inner game had led to success on the diamond.

As I lay sleepless on my cot that night, I rehearsed again and again in my mind, not only my big hit, but the mental events which had preceded it. I clearly saw that the pain of my pre-game torments—the agony of the last day and a half—was of my own creation. I had put myself through all that anguish need-lessly. I also clearly saw what effect that last-minute victory *inside* had had on the baseball game *outside.*

I had learned something. Something monumental. I had had a taste of the relationship—and even the command—that my inner world had on my outer. That was the moment I began to realize that each one of us has a lot to say about what happens in our respective worlds, and that much of what we experience in life is of our own creation.

This breakthrough was confirmed the very next week. We were now into the three-game series with the Indians. My first at bat was a bad experience. My inner game was in full swing, and I lost. I started thinking that Troy Scott would *really* be out to get me now. I had gotten the game-winning double off him, and he was not going to take it amicably. I had it all con-structed in my mind how he was going to bean me right in the head this time, to teach me a lesson. I made three pathetic waves at the pitches he threw and gladly sat down on the bench. I had struck out, but at least I still had my life.

As I sat there on the bench, I had this gnawing feeling in my stomach that I had turned coward again. I had reverted back to my rookie traits of letting the inner game get away from me. It all came back to harrow me up once again. "Never again," I decided, "Even if I don't get a hit, I'm going to stand in there and take solid cuts at good pitches. No jumping back, no diving away, no more just going through the motions of being a batter. Get over the fear," I demanded, "and really attack the pitch."

We went on to win the series in the third game. I got several hits, including another clutch double off Troy Scott. Once again it had been confirmed. I had seen clearly that in the game of baseball the major determinant in how well I played had been my mind management. And I began to suspect that it reached well beyond baseball.

As time went on I noticed that others before me had seen this great truth. Seemingly everywhere I turned some insightful person had also recognized that our lives are the product of our thoughts. I had read Solomon's declaration in the Bible, "As a man thinketh in his heart, so is he;" and heard the statement from Emerson, "The ancestor of every action is thought;" and from Buddha, "All we are is a result of what we have thought."

My respect for the mind with all its freedom and powers grew; and I often pondered the premise, "My life is the product of my thoughts." But, not until I began to take that principle literally, until I began to see how exactly I create my world with my own thoughts, did I begin to fully appreciate the *magnitude* of the power packed in that concept. Recognizing that, I began to study the principles of the mind more diligently, to apply them in my own life, as well as to teach and document the results of what mind management has done for thousands of others.

I hope that these pages will prompt you to give more thought to thinking, and motivate you to sharpen your skills in mind management and unlock the simple mystery of how to empower your life, thus winning the game of life on all levels.

By mastering the principles described in the coming chapters, you will attain a level of control over yourself and the world outside that at times will astound you. As you grow in your appreciation for the power of mind management, you will wield that power more artfully and judiciously than ever before. Greater success and deeper satisfaction will be yours as a result.

One of my main objectives in writing this book is to lay so much evidence in front of you that you will not be able to turn away from that truth. I want you to believe—believe in yourself and know that you have power, and you can do it. You can become the very person you want to become.

When we fully comprehend how precisely everything, from our character to our circumstances, represents the exact replication of what we have created in our minds, it stands among the most monumental and empowering revelations a being can receive.

CHAPTER 2

Mental Creation

The power of thought is the power of creation. Thoughts are not just airy vapors; they are packets of formative energy. They exert direct effect upon your body, your behavior and even the external world around you.

Your internal environment has power over your external environment. You have tremendous control. You can alter circumstances and events at will by first creating a vision of what you want to have happen and then giving yourself permission to enact it.

People are only victims of circumstance if they believe that they are and take a passive position, letting their lives be subject to outside forces.

Moment by moment, thought by thought, you author your own script. You do it actively or passively. Either way, you are ultimately the cause determining which effects occur.

Each one of us stands as a creative force of immense potency and potential. Believing that truth is half the battle.

Ernest Holmes, Ph.D., philosopher and author, said:

> As God's thought makes worlds and peoples them with all
> living things, so does our thought make our world and
> peoples it with all the experiences we have had. By the
> activity of our thought things come into our life, and we are
> limited because we have not known the truth; we have
> thought that outside things controlled us, when all the time
> we have had within that which could have changed
> everything and given us freedom from bondage.

THE DUAL CREATION OF ALL THINGS

Every human accomplishment goes through two creations. There comes first a mental creation, the spawning and
development of an idea. That idea becomes a blueprint and a
directive which the body follows to produce the second creation,
the physical or behavioral creation.

People rise or fall, limp or leap, cower or conquer,
dependent on the degree of their mind management. The
moment you start thinking differently, the world changes. A new
mental creation precipitates a new physical or behavioral
creation. The effects are often amazingly rapid. People can
make dramatic, stunning changes in short order by simply
altering their thoughts.

The truly exciting part of their transformations lies in the
astounding discoveries they make regarding their abilities and
capacities. They realize that the potential has been there all
along, and so have the opportunities, but their own thoughts have
been holding them back. When they see that it has been *only*
their thoughts which have been holding them back, galaxies of
potential open up to them. Suddenly they see—and seize—the
opportunities which have been staring them in the face all along.

A COUCH POTATO COMES TO LIFE

I submit, as a representative case, Priscilla Welch. If you are not into running, particularly the marathon event, you may have never heard of Priscilla Welch. She is an inspiring human being. Her active life prompts other people to examine their own, causing them to see that opportunities and limitations are what they make of them.

At age 34, Priscilla, who comes from Great Britain and now lives in Boulder, Colorado, characterized herself as the classic "couch potato." Out-of-shape and overweight, she had never been athletic in her life. At one time she had been a two-pack-a-day smoker.

Then, in 1979, at almost 35 years old, she decided to change all that. She made up her mind to get off the couch, lose some weight and become a lot more active in her life. She took up the sport of running.

The beginning was modest. The day she laced on her first pair of serious running shoes she was not a world-class runner. The thought hardly crossed her mind. "I had no plans to reach a competitive level. That just came with progress and was a complete surprise to me."

Priscilla's first "surprise" came in 1980. Finishing second in a major 10K race, her confidence blossomed. She began to think bigger, contemplating greater feats, like running a marathon. (Running has that great inherent quality: It begs you to measure and surpass yourself.)

Running a marathon, a distance of 26.2 miles, is a definitive statement in dedication and discipline. Competitive runners scorch the course at a rate of 5 to 5.5 minutes a mile. Anyone who sets such a goal confronts an army of self-doubts. Priscilla Welch confronted hers, called their bluff, and made a firm promise. She set her mind; she was going to run a marathon. And she kept that promise.

Her first marathon did not make headlines. Yet, a crucial milestone had been reached. That day her vision of herself expanded. She knew she had done something difficult, something not in her nature. Whatever it had done for her physically, inside she knew she was a stronger, more competent human being. Most importantly, she sensed that greater things were possible.

Priscilla had caught a glimpse of her capabilities. Her expectations climbed and so did her performance. One by one, new commitments were made and then kept.

In 1984, the United States hosted the Summer Olympic games. In Los Angeles, California there was, for the first time in Olympic history, a women's marathon. At age 39, Priscilla Welch was there—*not standing* on the curb, waving and urging her countrywomen on to victory. Rather, she was one of the Olympian competitors, running a fiercely valiant race. Competing against the best in the world, she burst across the finish line at 2:26.51! She had broken personal barriers, taken sixth place in the Olympic Marathon, set a British national record, and impressed the world!

VICTORY BEGETS VICTORY

Analysts and reporters made a big deal of her age. Priscilla downplayed it. "People," she stated, "are just beginning to wake up and realize that at age 40 to 45 you've still got it. I think we are all programmed early to accept limitations... We're brainwashed completely about age, and it's a lot of garbage."

To prove that point, she just kept running. In 1987, eight years after her first race, Priscilla Welch, the former couch potato, entered the New York Marathon. Pounding through the boroughs and across the bridges, she ran the socks off of women half her age. And, that day, at age 42, bless her ancient heart, she won it!

Priscilla is a shining example of a profoundly significant truth: The ultimate determinant in human performance is the state of mind. It is the vision and the faith—the ability to believe empowering thoughts—that matters most. Physical conditioning is a huge factor but not the greatest. In the final analysis, victory in life is a mental accomplishment.

The truly exciting thing to contemplate about Welch and others like her is where they came from and how they got to the pinnacles of lofty goals. They were not born champions.

One day, during one of my seminars, I had related the stories of Priscilla Welch and a couple of other exceptional performers. A woman raised her hand and commented, "Most of us in this room are just ordinary people. You keep telling us about all these 'High Achievers'."

This gave me the opportunity to make a crucial point. "Yes," I responded, "Priscilla Welch can *now* be considered a high achiever. But she didn't know she would accomplish all that, and neither did anyone else, when she started out. Priscilla began as an 'ordinary person' and *became* a high achiever."

Greatness isn't something you're born with, it's something you create and develop. She became exceptional, not with a perfect foreknowledge, but only with the decision to do something better and the courage to commence. It was *during— and because of*—the stretching process that Priscilla *discovered* how much ability she really had. She learned to believe in herself, to overcome self-doubts and to harness and focus her inner strength.

Priscilla Welch *became* a champion, incrementally, a step at a time, by managing her thoughts! She learned and verified the grand secret: **High achievers are ordinary people who discover that ordinary people have extraordinary potential.**

When a reporter asked, "Looking back to 1987, when you won the New York Marathon, what was your outlook going into the race? Did you think you had a chance to win?", she answered:

> I aimed for it and focused really well on it—I was so
> determined—and in the end I was amazed that it all paid
> off. It sort of frightens me even today; it's surprising what
> you put in your mind if you really want something. You put
> that goal deep into your subconscious, and when you
> actually get it, it's a little bit scary.

Priscilla Welch is only one example of how remarkably a life can be transformed through effective mind management. That which applies to her applies to you. Like Priscilla, first and foremost, **your** output, **your** productivity and **your** achievements are the outward manifestations of **your mind management.**

Those who awaken to the literal reality of mental creation enter a wondrous realm of growth, progress and continuous improvement because they can then take charge of so much. They can control the keyboard which determines what shows up on their screen, and can program success and happiness, rather than powerlessness and fear. They can see they are the cause and not just the "innocent victim" of all the effects exerted upon them. They gain the power to act, rather than to be acted upon.

The universe stands before each one of us, vast, malleable and full of potential. What you and I make of that immense potential depends largely on how well we grasp and apply this one grand truth:

WE ALTER OUR DESTINY
BY ALTERING OUR THOUGHTS.

Change your thoughts, and you change your world. It all begins in the mind.

CHAPTER 3

Definitions

It all begins in the mind. All human endeavor, achievement and accomplishment begins with a mental creation. Sounds simple enough, right? It is. And, yet, I feel pretty confident in telling you that you may not be getting the full benefit of those fundamental powerhouses of insight, because the waters of human performance have been so muddied and polluted with useless garbage, confusion reigns.

Let me offer an analogy. You have a terrific automobile, loaded with accessories and equipped with the most powerful engine available anywhere. Yet, you sense, the car is not performing at peak capacity. This baby is capable of a whole lot more.

Even a layman knows that if you seek higher performance from your car—to improve acceleration, go faster on the top end and improve the gas mileage—you would work on the source, the engine. You would get under the hood and make the corrections, tweaks and adjustments until that engine was hot and humming.

You would deem anyone a nut who, having the same objectives, would start fiddling around with the accessories, instead of working on the source of power. Tearing into the radio, studying the power door locks and staring into the rearview mirror to see where you've been, does not improve performance!

Yet, that is what all the human performance pollution I'm alluding to urges you to do. Authority figures from virtually every field have you focused on the upholstery and buttons of human performance, instead of the engine. And, to a fairly large degree, our generation has been buying into that emptiness.

THE TERRITORY

To get back to the source, we need to define "mind." This is no humble task. For centuries, sages and scientists have had good intentions but have wound up making the issue far more cloudy than clear.

Since the topic delves into the very essence of man, all branches of human concern have something to say. Religionists contend one thing, humanists another, and philosophers go bananas spouting theories. Unfortunately, most of the rhetoric has missed the mark. (They have inflated the value of the accessories while flattening the tires.)

Science has avoided the issue altogether, branding the term "mind" as unscientific. Until recently, most scientists have staunchly held that mind does not even exist. The very subject causes them to squirm like a den mother with a frog down her back. Life, in the eyes of science, is nothing more than the physiological operations within a collection of cells. Thought, consciousness and personality are merely products of the neuroelectricity and biochemistry of the brain. We're simply physical machines that just happen to think. Unfortunately, what that leads to is a focus on "brain" only. Studying the "gray matter" and the "white matter," science overlooks the most "crucial matter" of all.

Personally, though my degrees are in the exact sciences, I have never been able to accept science's position. If individuality and personality are just a matter of tissues and chemicals, and my neurons are essentially identical to yours (and everyone else's), and my brain uses the same chemicals as yours (and everyone else's), how come you and I (and everyone else) are so different and individually unique? Something other than "brain tissue" lies at the core of all this.

And, yet, if you agree that there *is* something to define, what do *you* want to name it? Consciousness, Soul, Spirit, Brain, Mind, Psyche, Ego-Id-Superego, Awareness, Self, Higher Self, Inner Self? The task presents bewilderment. Add to that all the connotative and denotative semantics that flow out of those terms, and you have a labyrinth that would have made the Minotaur dizzy.

PSYCHOLOGY DUCKS THE ISSUE

Even the science of psychology (which claims to be the very finest, fully-equipped, service department) renders no help. (Check the rear-view mirror one more time, Sigmund.)

If you asked the man on the street, "Which branch of science studies the mind?" he would likely reply, "Why, psychology, of course." That is, as a former professor of mine used to say, "the wrong misconception." (I always wanted to know what the right misconception was.)

The man on the street might think that psychology is "the study of the mind," but psychology formally disclaims that notion. Psychology uncourageously opts to define itself as the "Study of *Human Behavior.*" *

"True scientists" only believe in stuff they can see, you see. John Watson, one of the pillars of the behaviorist temple,

---

* Psychology does not define itself as we would expect, and as the Greek roots would suggest and beg for. "Psyche" is best translated from Greek into English as "soul," but is most popularly rendered "mind." "Logy," a derivative of "logia" in Greek and medieval Latin means "discourse or speech", signifies "the speech about" or "the doctrine or study of" a given subject. Fine then, you'd think it would be simple from here. Psychology should be just what the man on the street thinks it is—the Study of Mind. Instead, Psychology, defied its own root derivations and decided to call itself the "Study of Human Behavior."

argued that psychology must confine itself to *observable* events. Since we cannot *see* thinking or feeling or "the mind," we should not try to explain behavior in such terms. He actually declared that we did not need such "fuzzy" concepts to predict behavior. In effect, behaviorists (by their own definition) have declared their science to be "mindless."

This self-selected definition creates a self-imposed exile from the truth. Choosing to study the effect (behavior) while disregarding the cause (mind), Watson, and others like him, have walled themselves off from any valid progress. In essence, they have propped their cars up on blocks so they could spin their wheels really fast.

Nevertheless, behavioral scientists vociferously claim to be delving into the very heart of what makes us tick. (Or, in some cases, tic.) How can psychology claim to be authoritative on the effects of the mind when it rejects the existence of mind in the first place? That's like pretending to explain the origin of applesauce after having repudiated the existence of apples. (The man dog-paddling in the water over there is John Watson. He missed the boat.)

IN SEARCH OF A PARADIGM

No wonder behavioral scientists have *under*whelmed us. Their foundation is cracked, so the whole building is shaky. The very definition of psychology prevents it from coming to the truth. If there was ever a branch of science in need of a paradigm shift, it is this one. In more than a century, this formal branch of science has failed to put forth a comprehensive explanation of human mental function and/or dysfunction.

When you hear of someone going to their physician to be treated for bronchitis, you have a pretty good idea of what will happen. A culture will be taken, a pathogen will be identified and the appropriate antibiotic will be prescribed. There is a fairly uniform standard of care because medicine has a working theory which unifies cause and effect.

Poor old psychology can not do that because it has no underlying working theory upon which to base diagnosis and treatment.

When you hear of someone going in for treatment for mental illness, is it going to be an encounter group, cozy chats with a goateed man in a white lab jacket, injection of some drugs, yoga, electrical shock treatment or simply a frontal lobotomy? What is called "treatment" is a craps shoot. It varies with every institution and every practitioner.

The words "mental illness" are taboo these days. The reason is simple: If you talk about illnesses, you need to talk about cures. Cures in psychology and psychiatry are ambiguous. We're all appalled by the all-too-common reports of deviants who have been "cured" by eminent behavioral authorities, who have immediately gone out and raped, maimed or murdered another innocent victim. So, "cures" are downplayed, and everyone tiptoes by the skeleton in the closet and talks about "dysfunction." We will continue to reap this low-grade harvest until we improve what is sown. Psychology will never get a handle on the effects until it recognizes the cause.

When you get to the bottom line, psychology argues that mankind is mindless. They say we are either pushed by dark, suppressed, sexual forces or pulled along like puppets on the strings of environment and outward stimuli. They paint us into a corner of utter powerlessness.

Where, in that tug-of-war, do our own thoughts, our own decisions, our own judgments enter in? Where do courage, commitment, integrity and perseverance play a role? Psychology closes its eyes and ears to the truth that human beings are independent, thinking entities with the power to rise above animal drives, instincts and environment.

Certainly, culture and environment exert huge influence, but they do not *make* us what we are. Our current culture, for good or for bad, is a factor and not the determinant, unless we allow that to be the case.

We think!   And with those thoughts we shape our behavior. The world is replete with examples of people who have rejected all sorts of external stimuli, who have broken down barriers in the pursuit and achievement of goals of their own device, despite what environment, society or the zodiac decreed. Why? Because they took command and made up their *minds* to do so.

DEFINING BRAIN

Let me now cut to the "chase scene" and define "brain" and "mind," integrating the broad gamut of evidence. These ideas are founded in ancient wisdom, reaffirmed by modern research and corroborated by productive results in the lives of successful people.   They are consistent with common knowledge, common experience and common sense.

Let me start with something that science, religion and philosophy can all agree on, the definition of brain. This is universal; everyone agrees that there is an organ called the brain. (This is accepted even by those people who don't use one.)

Brain: The portion of the vertebrate central nervous system that constitutes the organ of thought, sensory interpretation and neural coordination, that is made up of neurons and their processes, that is enclosed within the skull, being continuous with the spinal cord through the foramen magnum and with the cranial nerves.

Here, then, stands our working definition for the term "brain." Brain is the grand organ, the master control center of all that is body. Research institutes worldwide are intently studying the properties of brain and how it functions. The coming decades are going to cast much light, adding to our understanding of how we function neuroanatomically and neurophysiologically. Yet, I still hold that the biomechanics of the brain are not what constitute mind.

Each time I sort through this issue, I arrive at essentially the same conclusion as that of respected researcher and author Dr. Barbara Brown:

> But finally I, too, have come to the conclusion, and quite analytically and logically I believe, that the scientific consensus that mind is only mechanical brain is dead wrong. I have become reasonably convinced...that the research data of the sciences themselves point much more strongly toward the existence of mind-more-than-brain than they do toward mere mechanical brain action. I believe I can make a solid case for the existence and potential of a superior intelligence within every man, a mind born of brain but existing apart from brain, a mind with extraordinary, unacknowledged potency and range of powers.

DEFINING MIND

Mind and brain are not synonymous. Mind, the great producer, is not a product. It is much more than the electrochemical workings of neural tissue. Brain, the master organ of the body, is not the ultimate center or core of the person or personality. The brain is not our essence, but mind is. Brain, rather, is the organic cloak, a garment, worn by mind, and used temporarily to further its progress.

In the statement above by Dr. Brown, I would alter one word. She says that within every person there is "a mind born of brain." I would supplant "born" with "borne." Mind is not an offspring of brain, rather it is borne of brain, or, in other words, "carried," supported and furnished with means of expression, by brain.

Mind is the specific, intelligent entity each of us recognizes as the very essence of self—the individual, personal, self-aware being of intelligence which, in the deepest sense, is the essential "me" within. Each of us has a clear, ever-present, conscious awareness of what is "me" and "not me," of what is "in here" versus "out there." I use the term "mind" synony-mously with that conscious awareness. They are one; not only inseparable, they are the same.

Mind is the INTELLIGENCE, the very self, the self apart from gross corporeal substance. This intelligence is capable of growth, enlargement, continuous improvement and limitless pro-gression. Ironically, I believe the Greeks were pretty close with their choice of the word, "psyche," which best translates into English as "soul." Your intelligence is not immaterial; it is a self-existent material entity which can exist, and is totally capable of thought, separate from the body. The Greeks knew that, too. I marvel at how insightful and accurate Plato was, and I support his point unreservedly: "Thinking is the soul talking to itself."

When the "psyche" leaves the body, the body along with the brain inside it, dies.

Death is not a rare phenomenon; it happens all the time. So do near misses. A goodly number of people, more than many of us realize, have had a near-death experience (NDE). These people have provided insight which is beyond price. They define death as none other than the intelligence (mind) exiting the body. NDErs declare that they—their unique personality and individ-uality—are not obliterated at death. Neither is the conscious, thinking portion of them radically revised or altered. They continue to understand just as before, to think as they did, to believe as they did, to love who they did and in every way continue to totally identify with who they have been and still are.

Their mind with its incessant thinking ability persists, totally separate from the body, entirely intact. In other words, it is possible to be "out of your body" and even "out of this world," but you can never be "out of your mind."

In summary, I reiterate: Mind is not a product of brain nor any other physical source. Mind is the independent, self-existent INTELLIGENCE which is uniquely you. You—your inner self—are what I call mind. You are it, and it is you. Your mind is capable of enlargement. Intelligence can be added to your intelligence. In fact, you hunger for it. There is, deeply inherent in all of us, a great inner need to grow, expand and improve. The extent of this advancement has no upper bounds. As implied above, not even the bounds of mortal life can hold us back from this journey of continuous improvement. Unlimited potential is not a hollow superlative. It is an apt description of your very nature. As the universe is infinite, so are you.

You, my friend, are inseparable from your thoughts. Mastering them is the greatest of all quests, for you are mastering yourself. The very purpose and essence of existence itself is mind management—progressing inevitably to total mind mastery. When that occurs, not even the elements nor the energies of the universe can decline to be your stewards.

CHAPTER 4

The Matter of Thought

Thoughts are real. They are not ethereal figments; they are organized energy. The reality of our thoughts and their effects were described in poetic terms by Henry Van Dyke:

> I hold it true that thoughts are things;
> They're endowed with bodies, breath and wings;
> And that we send them forth to fill
> The world with good results, or ill.
>
> That which we call our secret thought
> Speeds forth to earth's remotest spot,
> Leaving its blessing or its woes
> Like tracks behind it as it goes.
>
> We build our future, thought by thought,
> For good or ill, yet know it not.
> Yet, so the universe was wrought.

While you probably agree with Van Dyke's gist, it's possible you may not be taking his statements literally enough. Again I say, thoughts are real! They are concentrated bundles (quanta, if you will) of energy, capable of harnessing every other form of energy.

Thoughts are not only powerful, *they are, in fact, power.* Literally. Van Dyke, in case you missed it, said that even the universe was wrought (created) by thought. And I agree.

EINSTEIN'S INSIGHT

Let me offer you a quick confirmation about the reality of thoughts substantiated from current scientific insights. We are all familiar with Einstein's colossal breakthrough, expressed in the most sublimely succinct formula in all of mathematics and physics: $E = mc^2$. Yet few realize what that marvelous equation really means. Stated verbally, Einstein said that energy and mass (matter) are directly related. In fact matter and energy are actually different forms of the same thing. In point blank terms, energy *is* matter, and matter *is* energy.

The book in your hand, while seemingly solid, is made of molecules. Molecules can be broken down into atoms. In turn, atoms are composed of subatomic particles, protons, neutrons and electrons. From this point on, the subject becomes almost mind-boggling in its intricacy, and I will greatly simplify. The bottom line is that, subatomically, the world is composed of very small, highly energized particles which are difficult to describe, but are best viewed as vibrating energy. In Einstein's own words, "Energy has mass, and mass represents energy."

An infinitely comprehensive law of conservation prevails in the universe, and Einstein grasped it. Matter cannot be created out of nothing; neither can it be "destroyed." The same holds true of energy. Energy cannot be annihilated. One reality (matter or energy) can be converted to the other, but neither can be destroyed. The total amount of mass-energy in the universe never changes.

Matter represents a configuration of energy, and energy can be correctly viewed as a form of matter. Light, the epitome of this principle, quavers at the border of two states, matter and energy. For years physicists wrestled with that issue. They could not discern whether light was a form of energy (because it had wave properties) or a form of matter (because it had particle properties). The answer was "Yes!" Light is both—energy and matter. In fact, it is energy-matter. And so are your thoughts!

Thoughts are degrees of light, invisible to the physical eye; a concept which we plainly and repeatedly infer in common figures of speech. Customarily, after grasping a new idea, we say that we've been "enlightened." Therefore, if thoughts are forms of light, they are quanta of energy-matter and should exhibit simultaneously the properties of waves and particles.

We have known for decades that the brain is a transmitter of energy which we measure in terms of waves. Brain waves have been gauged, quantified and classified. Of recent vintage, Dr. Frank Duffy has produced a device called a BEAM scanner. BEAM is the acronym for Brain Electrical Activity Mapping. With such devices, scientists measure different states of mind and the performance of the brain in its many functions.

From this and a multiplicity of other sectors, science validates that thoughts are forms of energy and, if energy, then they are also matter.

We are only beginning to scratch the surface of our ability to measure the mind. Someday we will discover more accurate ways of measuring this energy and will find that it is the highest form of energy on the spectrum. Have we not already demonstrated that empirically? Through the power of thought, mankind has already harnessed other potent forms of energy to an impressive degree. It remains only a matter of time and development until we harness them all. This is nothing more nor less than a case of the lesser becoming subject to the greater.

Now, you are probably asking, "Does all this matter?" (Pun intended.) Yes! Thoughts are just as tangible and just as real as the chair, sofa or bed you are relaxing on as you read this book. Yet, thoughts have amazing properties, excelling most energy-matter.

Much more needs to be written on this topic, and I will do so later on in the book. For now, center on the realization that thoughts are literal forms of energy. And this energy can be focused and directed, and has supremacy over all other forms of energy and matter. Furthermore, your ability to control and wield this power can grow and increase. Your ability to do so is a measurement of and proportionate to your current level of faith and internal strength or in other words your level of mind management.

Returning now to Van Dyke's assertion that this is none other than the power by which even God creates is both awe-inspiring and humbling. Yet, once the initial shock wave passes over us, the simple beauty and correctness of that thought distills upon our hearts, and reason and logic confirm it. Hope and gratitude ensue; and so does an immense source of strength.

UNLIMITED BY NATURE

Understanding that we as lowly mortals can develop the same mechanisms of creation by which "the universe was wrought" need not be a thought which either diminishes Deity or overly-enshrines mankind. When rightly viewed, the concept inspires us to due diligence and provides greater impetus for taking responsibility for living better lives. When we see that, sloth, indifference and the squandering of such inestimable potential, become unjustifiable and intolerable.

The rate and magnitude of your growth is self-determined. You can dig in your heels and adamantly refuse to proceed. Or, you can slam the accelerator to the floor and break all previous records. It's entirely up to you.

Ultimately, your limits are self-imposed. Inherently, there are none. I state that because I hold that we are literally children of God, created in the exact image and likeness of the Infinite Being. And if God be infinite then so must be his off-spring.

We don't realize who we are and are virtually blind to the extent of our celestially-endowed powers and eternal potential. Our underappraisal consequently leads to underperformance.

In this temporal world, every living species manifests an obvious principle. Every child has, encoded in the very nature of its being, all the characteristics, capacities and potentials of its parents. Offspring duplicate parents. They start out as weak, undeveloped types of their progenitors, but they do not stay that way for long. Growing and developing, they gradually and inexorably become likenesses of their forebears.

This one truth is seen throughout all of nature: Everything reproduces after its own kind. Nothing is more universally validated in the natural, divinely-created universe than that principle. Where was there ever a mother who was not first a daughter? And where was there ever a father who was not first a son? The offspring of every species is created in the image and likeness of its parents, and passing through stages of development each son becomes like his father with similar capacities, attributes and characteristics.

All of this testifies of greater things. If you and I, the offspring of God, did not conform to that same universal pattern of nature, it would be the first and only exception in the universe, and the most egregious contradiction of law, logic and sense imaginable. We have the self-same capacities, potentials and traits possessed by our parent—an unlimited, ever-creating being—and they are fully developable within us. Who, more than men and women, God's most singular and lofty creations, should rightfully fulfill this law and conform to this principle?

We are all beings possessing, in varying degrees of refinement, the most unlimited and illimitable faculties. (!)

Your mind, a classic spark of Divine Intelligence itself, is capable of expansion and accomplishment beyond that which most people can believe. Ironically, it is that disbelief itself which prevents us from realizing that growth and development. It is disbelief in our vast potential which impedes us most. Until

we cast disbelief aside, not even God can circumvent it. You
alone have the authority to demolish that barrier, and when you
do, you will receive, accomplish or become so much more than
you now are.

Your mind is your most crucial resource, your crowning
asset and ironically can be your greatest nemesis and limiter.
One of the greatest twists of irony on the list of eternal principles
is the one which states: THAT WHICH IS YOUR GREATEST
STRENGTH MUST BE RESPECTFULLY GUARDED, FOR
IT CAN ALSO BECOME YOUR GREATEST FLAW.

Take control of this awesome resource. Cast out skep-
ticism and cynicism. Embrace belief, hope and confidence.
Reject fear and doubt—the parents of limitation. Open up to
faith, the precursor of continuous improvement. Exercise your
freedom to choose, and opt for growth!

Greatness is a choice. You enroll yourself and pursue the
course. Stop loitering in the eddies and alleys, and hit the super-
highway. William Jennings Bryan said it perfectly:

> Destiny is not a matter of chance, it is a matter of choice; it
> is not a thing to be waited for, it is a thing to be achieved.

Great lives don't just occur, they are sought for, and the
individual man or woman is the pivotal determinant in that
divinely-supported process.

CHAPTER 5

Infinite Possibilities

Great achievements happen because they are caused to happen. Every outstanding outward triumph is the manifestation of an equally outstanding inner triumph. There are absolutely no great victories manifest in the external world which were not, first, fought and won in the mind.

Whenever I think of great victories, one supreme example always comes to mind. Drawn from the annals of sport, classic elements of this story are both timely and timeless.

When Sports Illustrated published its Silver Anniversary Issue, it cited the 10 foremost sports accomplishments of the era it had been covering the sports scene. Then, preeminent above those, they hailed one feat as the greatest of them all—the running of the four-minute mile by Roger Bannister. The reason was not the physical feat alone, nor the tremendous mental victory for Bannister personally, both of which were prodigious accomplishments. That which so impressed Sports Illustrated was the transforming effect Bannister's achievement had on athletes in virtually every other sport.

In the early 1950s, Roger Bannister was a medical student at Oxford, England. Toiling in anonymity, he devoted himself to his medical studies and the mile event in track and field. At the outset, he was not considered to be a great runner. The British Commonwealth boasted of other runners who were rated ahead of Bannister. One was an Australian by the name of John Landy. Landy was considered to be the beamish boy of the British realm.

The world record they were all gunning for had been set in 1943. A Swede named Gunder Haegg had run the mile in 4 minutes, 1.4 seconds, and that record remained on the books for nearly 10 years. There was a mystique about the Haegg record. Gunder was tall and powerful. The day Gunder "the Wonder" set the record a reporter said, "It felt like the earth trembled;" and some people spoke of "maximum limits." Over the ensuing years, good runners came and went, none of them making an appreciable threat on Haegg's record. It began to be said around the track and field world that nobody ever would—that Haegg had run the ultimate mile.

By the early 1950s, medical authorities started chiming in. Respected anatomists and physiologists expressed grave doubts about the ability of the body to run a four-minute mile. The logic was plain: "It's a simple matter of physics. The human body is a machine with a limited work capacity, based on its component parts. The human body has only so many bones, muscles and sinews, and it just cannot propel itself over a mile distance in under four minutes." Bannister, a medical student, would have been attuned and exposed to such "evidence."

The situation boiled down to these elements: A long-standing record, mental barriers supported by authoritative sources, and an unheralded runner.

INNER CONVICTION

Roger Bannister did become a legend in his own time. He was knighted by the Queen, adored by the masses. But at first he drew little attention.

During the early months, people were not thronging Bannister, offering support and encouragement. No one was saying, "Roger, you're going to become one of the greatest runners of all time. You're going to do the impossible." The accolades would come after the fact. As is always the case, greatness was created in the solemn moments of his mind, well before the greatness was manifest to the world.

Bannister began by believing. He rejected the authoritative sources which denied the possibility. He built a belief system, added his own evidence, strengthened his own inner conviction. Bannister knew enough about human physiology to recognize a salient fact: The body is expandable! This great truth has far-reaching ramifications, and it applies not just to athletic performance.

Human beings are capable of growth and expansion! We are not static, rigid machines, bound by the way some metal die was cast. When you place demand on the human machinery and then balance that with a period of rest and recovery, the machinery, whether physical, emotional, intellectual, or spiritual, will expand. It grows stronger, and it enlarges its capacity. The progress becomes cyclical. Whenever a phase of demand is followed by a phase of recovery, the growth of the human machinery takes place. Administered in incremental doses, the growth and development will continue indefinitely.

Bannister understood this principle and based his pursuit upon it. Gradually, he achieved the confidence that Haegg's record could be broken. Then he moved ahead mentally and took direct aim on the seemingly impregnable four-minute mile barrier. "Without the concentration of the mind and the will, the performance would not result," he reflected.

UNFAVORABLE CONDITIONS

It all came down to May, 1954. On May 5th, it rained in Oxford, England. So, on May 6th, the track at Iffley field was wet and considered to be slow. Worse yet, the day of the race there was a cold, 15-mile-an-hour cross wind blowing, with occasional gusts up to 25 miles per hour just before the event began. Can't you picture the slim, sandy-haired Bannister preparing for the race, fighting a momentous mental battle? Just think of the avalanche of excuses he could have indulged in—the wet track, the cold cross wind. Even the setting itself had its drawbacks. Roger's first mile race as a freshman was at Iffley Road Track. It had been a very poor showing. Couple that with the haunting echoes of "experts" who were saying that what he was about to attempt was impossible, and you have an extraordinary clash.

In untrained minds, any one of the circumstantial excuses would have been sufficient for defeat. Bannister had become a giant through his concerted efforts, and he overrode the doubts and rationalizations. He decided that *he* was the biggest factor in the outcome of this race. As he walked to the starting line he said to himself, "There comes a moment when you have to accept the circumstances, and have an all-out effort, and I decided TODAY WAS THE DAY!"

FOUR LAPS TO GREATNESS

The conventional athletic track is a quarter mile in circumference. Thus the mile event comes down to four laps around the track. The gun went off, and the runners ran. At the end of the first lap Bannister was clocked at 57.5 seconds. At the end of the half-mile, the second lap, he was clocked at 1 minute, 58.2 seconds. That was a fast clip in those days. But it was in the third lap that the price would be paid.

As muscles burn oxygen beyond certain thresholds, lactic acid builds up in the muscle fibers, and pain is the result. Oh, how we humans despise pain. As pain mounts, so does the fierceness of mental battles. Repeatedly there comes the urge to slow down, to ease up. Looking back on those moments, Bannister stated, "The mental approach is one of the most important things in running. The man who can drive himself further once the effort gets painful is the man who will win."

Bannister stayed tough. As the pain and fatigue mounted, he kept battling. At the completion of the third lap, the record was within striking distance. He had won the battle of the third lap; the victory hung in the balance. Then came the fourth and final lap. As he rounded the first turn in the final lap, he faltered. The wet track momentarily became a factor. He thought for a split second that he was going to lose stride, stumble and fall to the track. His head throbbing, his lungs burning, voices welled up inside and said, "Ease up, Roger, you've just blown it. Settle back now and just take the win." Again, you see the MENTAL WARFARE.

Rather than slackening, he redoubled his efforts, fought off the pain and doubts, picked up his knees and drove into that second turn. After the turn, there was the long straightaway. He began an all-out sprint, leaving the field of runners behind. It was a spellbinding moment. One human being, pounding down that track, mouth open, head thrown back, bringing in all the oxygen he could to service that debt, he radiated something from his very presence. The people in the stands started to sense it. They realized that was greatness down there in front of them, that history was probably in the making. As though led by a choral leader, 1200 men, women and children rose to their feet to cheer him on. Their collective voice seemed to say, "Keep going. Don't quit. You're so close, keep fighting."

The final moments are best reported in his own words:

> In the last 300 yards of my record run, my mind took over. It raced well ahead of my body and drew my body compellingly forward. I felt that the moment of a lifetime had come. The world seemed to stand still. With 50 yards left, my body had long since exhausted all its energy, but it went on running just the same. The last few seconds seemed never-ending. I leaped at the tape like a man taking his last spring to save himself from the chasm that threatens to engulf him.

Bannister collapsed across the finish line into the arms of his coach, Thomas Kirk Cureton, and the clocks registered 3:59.4! He had done it! He had run the Miracle Mile!

A photograph of his final burst graced the cover of SI's Silver Anniversary Issue, and this was the headline:

> Somehow it does not seem that long ago....Roger Bannister, the man who did the impossible. In retrospect, it was Bannister's achievement that opened up the infinite possibilities of the years ahead. After that day at Oxford, ANYTHING SEEMED POSSIBLE.

That is why Bannister's achievement was cited as being the preeminent accomplishment of our times. He had seemingly opened up the "infinite possibilities of the years ahead." But in physical terms, had he really? No, a minute is still a minute, a mile is still a mile. What Bannister had done was overcome the barrier about barriers. He had proven that the limitation was not in the body. The experts were wrong. The limitation had not been in the body; it had been in the mind.

GREATER EVIDENCE

There remains a serious question as to whether there is any such thing as a maximum limit to the body. Bannister, who went on to become a physician, did not think so, and he placed the responsibility for that, not on the body, but the mind:

> The human spirit is indomitable. No one can say you must not run faster than this or jump higher than that. There will never be a time when the human spirit will not be able to better existing world marks. Man is capable of running a mile in three-and-a-half minutes.

One thing was sure, Bannister changed the world because he changed people's minds. "After that day at Oxford, anything seemed possible." Standing records in every endeavor in sport now stood in significant jeopardy of being broken. Athletes took heart. They thought differently, and a check of the record books of the time shows record after record being toppled.

Said Norman Cousins, "Each of us walks along the path of our own expectations," and this period of sports history bears that out. After record-setting performances, many champions of that era directly credited Bannister as the source of their inspiration. Roger Bannister had helped people to see and expect more. Thus they went ahead and did more.

It is the second chapter in the Bannister story which is the most compelling in the case for mind management. Do you know how long that great record lasted? Reflect with me, if you will. Gunder Haegg's record of 4:01.4 stood on the books for nearly a decade. On May 6, 1954, Roger Bannister surpassed that record, did what was said to be impossible. Amazingly, his record, the Miracle Mile, stood on the books for *barely a month!* You see, Bannister had overcome barriers in the minds of athletes in his own sport as well.

John Landy now knew that a four-minute mile was possible. Landy, like the rest of us, walked along the path of his own expectations. He was convinced that he was a better runner than Bannister. If Bannister could run the mile in under four minutes..."click"...Landy knew that he could, too.

Without watching one Jane Fonda workout video; without buying track shoes that could be pumped up; without breathing cleaner air; or eating sprouts, bee pollen or kelp; simply by changing his mind, John Landy erased Roger Bannister's name from the record book. Six weeks later, in Turkú, Finland, Landy, too, broke the four-minute-mile barrier. Furthermore, he bettered Bannister's mark by a full second, lowering the world record to 3:58 flat.

Both record-breaking performances, the great races of Landy and Bannister, hold one thing in common. They were first won mentally, then physically. So it is with you. Every one of your championship performances has resulted from your inner triumphs. As you continue to apply this principle correctly, nothing can keep you from going home with the gold. Circumstances have no power over you. Effects *always* follow causes.

SECTION II

THE EFFECT

If you mistake effects for causes, you cannot control either.

**BEHAVIOR IS MIND DRIVING BODY IN
FULFILLMENT OF DOMINANT THOUGHT.**

CHAPTER 6

Above Your Nature, Above Your Nurture

As a generation we are missing the point. Though massive evidence abounds, so many of us continue to discount the mental creation, attributing behavior instead to genetics, environment and/or conditioning. "It is your nature or your nurture, that makes you what you are," is the reheralded cry. This disempowering doctrine has been woven into our societal fabric. No one has to take fundamental responsibility for his or her life. Someone else or something else is always to blame.

In seminars I have retold the story of a disgruntled father in conference with a son who has brought home a less-than-stellar report card. "You're capable of straight A's," states the father, "and a B now and then is acceptable. But what is the reason for so many C's?" To this the son retorts, "I'm not sure myself, Dad. What do you think it could be, heredity or environment?"

Heredity and environment *are* major factors in human outcomes. Of that there is no question. Each exerts an influence, and the effects are significant. Yet, neither of those elements surpasses the influence of our own self-directed volition, the power of the human spirit.   Directed thought is the single, greatest determinant in human consequences.

FAULT LINES

Have you ever noticed how much excuse-making passes for truth? Join me on a brief, but all too common, excursion to the Land of Non-responsibility:

John is bright and well-educated.   He enjoys perfect health and possesses the ample energy of a fit 20-year-old. Holding down a job while attending the university, he demonstrates that he is not only capable but far from lazy. Personable and outgoing, John attracts friends easily. People like him.

Don't get me wrong, John, like everybody else, has his flaws. But we will just have to accept them and, more or less, learn to live with John the way he is. John, you see, is a red. No, not a communist, John is a red personality. That is why his mother, busy in her own life, writes his letters and thank-you notes. Reds are not thoughtful. They do not express their love and appreciation easily. It is not their nature. They are reds and that is the way reds are, you see. So now that we understand why John is the way John is, it makes it so much easier to relate to him. We can accept him and understand that when his grandmother sends him $1000 for his birthday, John doesn't need to express any appreciation, reds aren't inclined that way.

John's mother is a yellow.   Yellows love to spread sunshine and happiness wherever they go, and it is *natural* for them to want to write cheery little notes and cards. That is why John's mother writes his thank-you letter to his grandmother for him. It is her nature; it is not his.

Now that we know John's mother is a yellow, we can love and accept her, too. Of course, since she is a yellow, and it is her nature to write notes, if you ever get one from her, you need not be overly impressed, as though an independent, thinking human being decided of her own free will to thank you.

You should just chock it up to nature. The only reason she sent it was because it is her personality style. In essence, she had no choice; yellows can hardly keep themselves from gushing, you see.

Herb excels at leadership. Recently promoted to district vice president, he manages over 170 people and does it well. Of course, what would you expect? Herb is a Leo. Leos are natural born leaders. Mars, Jupiter and Saturn have tons to say about what kind of a leader you are.

How fortunate for Herb, who has always dreamed of being an effective manager, that he was born in late July. That made all the difference right there. Good thing he wasn't born in February, his goals of being a good manager would have never blossomed. The clouds shrouding Venus would have prevented it.

Had Herb wanted to be less forceful and dynamic, perhaps more of a conciliator, he would have been smart to have had himself born in late September or early October. That would have made him a Libra. Libras make great arbitrators. When the moons of Pluto (or is it Goofy?) line up just right, it helps folks seek harmony and peace. Whenever they sense tension, they fix it. That is the way Libras are, you know. The planets say so.

The idea that the planets guide our lives and shape our fate remains solid stuff. Such gospel has been known and taught for centuries.

If you have trouble accepting planetary control, it is probably because you are a second child. Second children are distrustful and cynical. Birth order is a crucial determinant in whether you are a skeptic or not.

People who are born second are virtually destined to be irreverent and disrespectful. How could they help it? From the time they were born into the precarious second position, they have been forced to wrest their parents' attention away from that self-centered, limelight-hogging first child who is a pleaser.

Being a first child makes you a sycophant. (Derived from the Greek word "psycho" and the Darwinian word "elephant.") You conform and perform because you have basked in the glow of your parents' doting attention from day one. Striving to maintain control of center stage, first children have a strong tendency, unfortunately, to become (uh-oh) Type-I personalities. I won't take time to list all the inbred traits you possess if you are a Type-I. You can't do much about them anyway. All your life your toxic environment has nurtured you into this syndrome, and you're stuck with those traits pretty much forever.

The only first children who do not express these tendencies are the ones who open and shut the womb simultaneously. Being an "Only Child" casts you into an even more restrictive mold. All of the horrible traits of all birth positions coalesce into making you a virtual Frankenstein of composite defects. You may as well go out and gargle with gasoline because everyone knows that an only child is destined for lassitude and ennui. They are classic underachievers in every case because life has just been too cushy for them. Everything has been given to them. Spoiled rotten from the start, no one doubts why they are such unmitigated messes. They couldn't help it. Look what their parents did to them.

Maybe you are feeling a bit left out because you are an eighth child and not many universities have conducted studies on "Eighth Child Post-kindergarten Neuro-bursitis." Do not despair. There are a bazillion other elements in your environment which you can accept as being the cause of your effects. Just give it a little thought and you will be able to come up with some hideous syndrome, all on your own, to account for all your rashes and pimples.

If it is not your *nature* to be a dud, you see, it is obviously then your *nurture*. You are a dud because your parents, den mothers and Little League coaches have conditioned you to be a dud. It just isn't your fault. You have faulty genes, unfavorable seating order in preschool and were born on one of your mother's bad hair days. And, besides that, everybody raised you wrong.

If you are detecting any sarcasm in these latest paragraphs, you are just overly suspicious. And if you are, please be reassured that it is not your personal responsibility. You are an insecure, suspicious, distrusting adult, because your "inner child" has been betrayed and deceived. Dysfunctional adults have troubles in life because they have troubled inner children, ranting around inside of them. (Here, all this time, you thought that rattling was a loose bolt in your pancreas.)

Well, as you can tell, I regret having to wrap up this little foray into Non-Responsibility-Land. It is such a comfortable place to be, and I was having so much fun. However, we need to climb out of this self-made swamp of excuses and clean up a bit.

THE DOCTRINE OF NON-RESPONSIBILITY

The great Hebrew leader, Joshua, said, "Choose you this day, whom ye will serve...," and I echo that request. It is time to make a choice. What will it be for you, Responsibility or Non-responsibility? You cannot have it both ways. Either you are a hapless product of genetics and environment wherein you accept the Nature-Nurture Doctrine as your constitution, or you accept the Doctrine of Agency and Responsibility.

You have guessed by now where I stand. I hold and declare that each of us stands as an independent agent, capable of rational thinking and the ability to make choices. When we make a choice, we also choose the consequences, and the responsibility lies squarely upon our own shoulders.

Contrastingly, the world is studded and strewn with excuses, and you can have any you want. From pop-psychology to the most sophisticated treatises from academia, they all boil down to a common bottom line: They are excuses.

Most of the books written on these "syndromes" propose to "increase awareness" so that you and I can understand and accept ourselves better. Not that they claim we can *do* all that much about them, but at least we know where to place blame. And in the final analysis that is what most people want out of those books anyway.

The Science of Psychology has proven itself to be little more than a prolific factory of scientific-sounding apologies. The vast majority of its vaunted theories preach the same doctrine: Non-responsibility. You need only select the flavor that suits your taste. But remember, no matter how valid, an excuse does not improve performance.

I know what I've written is going to make a lot of social scientists and liberal apologists angry with me, but (you guessed it) it's not my fault. I am a victim of my editor. She made me write this stuff. Send your venomous little epithets to Cecily Markland. I'm just this poor little author who has to write what he's told. (Besides, she is a blue, and blues are tough.)

Bluntly, and with all joking aside, the doctrine of non-responsibility is the most destructive ideology ever foisted onto mankind. Its origins date back to antiquity. In ancient Greece, the popular religion depicted capricious gods in charge of mankind's fate. "The gods say whether I live or die, whether I be ill or well, rich or poor, so why try?" The common man had no need to assume any responsibility. Helplessness was justified, everything was up to the gods.

Non-responsibility runs rampant in society today, so pervasive we hardly detect it. "The way I am is not my fault, and what happens to me is not within my control," echoes through the corridors of everyday conversations. "The men in my family have always been the kind that..." "This is just the way I am. I was born this way, and you cannot change that." "I've always been the type that..." "I've never been good at..." "My parents, my religion, my society, my government, my teachers (ad infinitum and ad nauseam) taught me to be like..." The list has no bounds, it could go on for ever.

The thought that we are cast in stone or "typed" is an impervious prison. It stands as one of the most disempowering ideologies one could ever entertain. It precludes improvement. No one improves if he or she believes that renovation is impossible.

THE LANGUAGE OF VICTIMIZATION

We see more advocacy of non-responsibility every day. Look no further than the main fare of the media. Journalists have done an absolutely superb job in helping us all see what a toxic society we live in. Hour after hour, program after program, viewers are bombarded with the description and accounts of victimized people. We sit there, absorb it and accept it at face value. In one way or another, each of us can place himself in one or more of the myriad syndromes of abuse. We can see that we have been wounded and mistreated. Since we have been abused, we conclude that what we do and who we are is not our fault. Not only can we dismiss responsibility for everything, we become convinced that it is our right to be compensated for all this misery. So we go out and find a lawyer to sue somebody.

I have no desire to minimize or trivialize or be insensitive to anyone who has been deeply wounded or mistreated or harmed. Some of us have been subjected to multiple abuses, some truly tragic and severe. We live in a toxic, imperfect environment and the casualties mount. Sociological, psychological, cultural, financial, sexual, political and environmental abuse abounds. There remains no question of that, and there is virtually no end to the list. It is appropriate and important to increase awareness and amend these breaches. The abuse and harassment have definitely got to stop.

Yet there stands one major point, above all else: It is our own *victimization thinking* which victimizes us the most.

Louis W. Sullivan, Secretary of Health and Human Services in the Bush Administration, stated:

> For young people growing up in otherwise unfavorable circumstance, values pave the road out of poverty. The tragic truth is that the language of "victimization" is the true victimizer—a great crippler of young minds and spirits. To teach young people that their lives are governed—not by their own actions, but by socioeconomic forces or government budgets or other mysterious and fiendish forces beyond their control—is to teach our children negativism, resignation, passivity and despair.

It follows that when we teach dependency on governmental and bureaucratic programs, we set the stage for disaster. Unfulfilled political promises yield disappointment; frustration ensues. Unresolved frustration leads to total disdain for the system and violence results.

The greatest antidote for this epidemic is the doctrine of individual responsibility. Nobody said it better than the late Dr. Benjamin Elijah Mays, former president of Morehouse College:

> It is not your environment, it is you—the quality of your mind, the integrity of your soul, the determination of your will—that will decide your future and shape your life.

ONE WAY OR THE OTHER

So choose. I invite you to join me on a quest for something greater—the living of an empowered life where you see yourself as a creative force and where you hold yourself accountable for what you create.

The way is not "comfy." We will not be spending any time sucking on the pacifier of non-responsibility. This book teaches what you must *do* to change, grow and improve your life, not where to affix blame. I am not even going to ask you to blame yourself; that is no more productive than the non-responsibility tripe.

I encourage you to rise above all the outside factors and forces, to see that they only hold you captive if you allow them to. I urge you to see yourself as a strong, independent entity, something above, and more powerful than, circumstances around you.

Most importantly, I plead with you to take a hard look at the law of cause and effect, and discern the crucial difference between those two elements. Most of what "shows up" in the world around you is an effect which has been caused by your thoughts.

You are not your emotions. You have them, but you are not your emotions. You are above them. Emotions are effects, not causes.

You are not your body. You have one, but you are not your body. Body is a factor, not a cause. You are greater than your physical form.

You are, above all these things, the force of causation which deals with factors, molding and shaping them into outcomes created by your choices. And, you are such a powerful cause, most of the effects you experience are of your personal production.

Knowing what is cause and what is effect provides access to the whole creative equation—the freedom and impetus to rise above current circumstances, current performance and current obstacles to ever-expanding vistas of progression and accomplishment.

CHAPTER 7

Above Your Body,
Above Your Blues

Body is a factor, not a cause. When the mind commits, the body responds. As valuable and as magnificent as it may be, the body is subservient to the mind. Shortcomings in the body, even devastating injuries, can be offset by strong states of mind—faith, determination and perseverance. Renee Riddle is one of several people who have demonstrated that.

Renee Riddle teaches hearing-impaired children. Holding a master's degree in Deaf Education, she is one of the brightest instructors in her field. In addition, she is blond and beautiful, a delight to be around. She inspires everyone who knows her. Someone once remarked to me that to be in her presence is a spiritual experience.

I knew Renee when she was growing up. Active and positive, she was a real participant in life. She loved softball and swimming and doing the things which teenagers love to do.

Between then and now, a significant event took place in her life. Renee doesn't play softball any more because she is paralyzed from the 11th thoracic vertebra down.

An accident occurred just after her graduation from high school. She had been swimming and was driving home to get ready for a softball game. She was in a bit of a hurry, and along the way she took her eyes off the road. In a split second, she lost control of her vehicle. It left the road, rolled over two or three times, and Renee's spinal cord was severed. The whole tragic accident took place in a handful of seconds. (Sometimes it's hard to believe that something so brief could have such long-lasting repercussions.)

For the first two weeks after the accident, she was in so much pain that she couldn't think about anything else. Even with heavy doses of morphine, Demerol and Valium, the pain was excruciating. So acute was the misery that the slightest vibration sent waves of pain through her body. It hurt to just have someone walk into her hospital room. The clumping of one nurse's wooden clogs was particularly agonizing for Renee.

During this time, being so subdued by the drugs and the pain, she didn't communicate much. Her parents were not sure what her reaction might be, and they posed a lot of questions to her doctor. He said, "It will be entirely up to Renee. It won't be the injury but the underlying attitude that will determine the future."

Renee is a success and an inspiration. She has faced the adversity and has handled it. She rarely gets down. From the time of the accident, she was the one who was giving encouragement to the people around her. One of Renee's best friends came to visit her in the hospital shortly after the accident. Upon seeing the limp, immobile figure that Renee was, she became so nauseous she threw up on the floor. Without uttering a word, she ran out of the room in tears. But Renee didn't get down, or feel sorry for herself, or curse the circumstances, or quit.

There were months of rehabilitation. In some ways, she had to start all over again—she had to learn how to sit up, using the muscles she was still able to control. Gradually, she improved. Then, and now, she's making it!

Renee's inner world conquered her outer. Renee Riddle fought her way back. She went on to college, obtained her bachelor's degree, and then her master's. Now she blesses the lives of hearing-impaired children in Salt Lake City, Utah.

SAME PERSON, DIFFERENT BODY

I have learned a lot from Renee Riddle. Her perspectives carry a great deal of weight with me. When I asked her how she dealt with everything when it really hit home that she'd never walk again, this is what she said:

> I realized that I had essentially three choices. One, I could kick, scream and refuse to accept it, and then drop out. Or two, I could do it, grumbling and hating life all the way. Or three, I could accept it, go on with my life and do it. For me, there was never really any question. I was going to go on. MY *LIFE* HADN'T CHANGED, JUST *MY BODY!*

That is powerful, if not profound. Renee's life had not changed, just her body! Circumstances were different—significantly different. But her life wasn't. She was still the same person and she had the same *life*. She said:

> One day I was talking with my brothers and I could see that not even my goals had changed. Before the accident I'd had three major goals: I wanted to go to college; I wanted to get married; and I wanted to have a family. And that hadn't changed because I was hurt. Even though the circumstances had changed, I was still the same person, and I was still going to reach my goals.

Whenever I think of Renee, I think of my company's logo, the American Clipper ship on the high seas, and I think of these words:

YOU CANNOT CONTROL THE WINDS IN LIFE,
BUT YOU DO REGULATE YOUR SAILS.

Renee Riddle conquers because she has chosen to conquer. She encountered some cruel winds, but she has maintained her course and she will achieve her destination just as surely. The voyage may take a bit longer, she may have to take a different course, but the outcome will be just as certain, and undoubtedly, even more rewarding.

For every Renee Riddle, you can find another individual who has chosen a different way. I know a paralyzed man who lives life seething venom and bitterness. His physical disability is no worse and no better than Renee's. Yet the outcomes are poles apart. One chooses pity, and the other chooses active living.

It comes down to an important distinction in their thoughts. Renee Riddle succeeds where the other person does not because she somehow grasped a crucial insight: She is not her body.

The bitter one does not make that differentiation. He, in essence, thinks, "My body is damaged; therefore, I am damaged." He does not see that he is separate from and far greater than his physical form. He can grow, contribute and progress. He can create happiness despite his physical form. He is not his body, and you are not yours. You are superior to— above—your body.

If I were to cut off your big toe, wouldn't you be essentially the same person? If it were your foot or your leg that was taken, would any part of your mind or personality or character be taken with it? No, you would still be there, the self-same person, undiminished. The essential YOU would still be intact. You are not your body. You are so much more.

Often we will so identify with our bodies that what our body feels is what we accept as our state of being. If our body is tired or sore or weak, we just go along with that. If we wake up feeling somewhat ill, and we have several distasteful projects in front of us, we can really "get into" being sick. Some of us are even fairly adept at *creating* sickness. Teenagers are masters of the art, and they can develop truly convincing flu symptoms and can even cough up blood to avoid taking a test at school for which they are unprepared.

We can all smile and relate to that. There have been times when I have been ill and, when it has been to my "advantage," been able to really identify with and amplify the sickness. Conversely, when I have had something very exciting or important to do, I can bail out of bed and be where I want to be, overriding my illnesses to a large degree.

There are examples which are less humorous than the "teenage morning sickness" syndrome. Unfortunately, there are people who create illness to avoid coping with other issues in their lives.

Clearly, the most formidable battles are not mind over body, but mind over misconception. (Body simply responds to the outcome.)

MIND OVER EMOTIONS

Just as you are above your body, so are you captain of your feelings and your emotions. How you feel is also an effect of your thinking. How you interpret the outside world determines the serenity or turbulence of the inner world. Wally O. is a prime example of the power of mind over emotion.

Wally O. had come to one of my seminars in his mid-30s, taken notes, stored away some of the principles, and gone on with life. In his 20s, Wally O. had earned two bachelor's degrees, one in interior design and the other in graphic design. Now married, he made the decision to go to graduate school and seek a master's degree in interior design with the goal of becoming a college professor and teaching.

Despite not working in interior design for quite some time, Wally O. was one of six, out of 169 applicants, accepted into the program. He received a teaching assistantship and a scholarship and seemed to be well on his way.

However, it is not unusual to find, on most faculties, certain members who take delight in applying unwarranted pressure on students to see if they can cull the crop of degree seekers. Wally O. found himself in a swamp infested with such crocodiles. Advisers on the thesis committee dumped intimidating, discouraging distortions about the rigors required for a successful thesis. Other professors applied their tactics, loading the graduate students up with insurmountable assignments, deadlines and expectations.

Unfortunately, at that time, Wally O. did not have the internal skills to cope with the pressures, and he let the faculty's "mind games" prey upon his confidence. Dwelling on the negatives, he became increasingly doubtful about his eventual graduation. Feeling overwhelmed, he grew despondent. Things unravelled from there, and Wally O. wound up in a psychiatric ward.

Wally O. was stabilized with the use of well-prescribed medication, which allowed him to come to equilibrium. Most effective courses of treatment for clinical depression combine medical support with mind management counseling. When the patient is stabilized, and they have gained control through mind management, the medical support can be withdrawn. The patients can then go on to complete independence.

At the hospital, Wally O. received wise counsel which awakened slumbering truths he had packed away. In his initial session, the counselor placed the responsibility for success and happiness on Wally O.'s shoulders. He was told that his dismissal date was his decision. Only he could effectuate "the cure." Only he could eject "the demons" of anxiety, perceived pressure, feelings of inadequacy, and fear of failure from his life. The counselor said, "You've got to take control of your thoughts."

Those words, Wally O. said, brought back the flood of principles and concepts of mind management which he had received in my seminar. He called his spouse that afternoon and requested that she find the notebook he had used. By that night Wally O. was reviewing his notes, filling his mind with the concepts which I call "dominant thought management" and "power goaling."

Before he closed his eyes in sleep that night, he had realized that he needed to clearly define his goal and focus on what he wanted to have happen, rather than what might go wrong. That night Wally O. resolved to concentrate on his graduation and force his fears out of his mind. He realized that all his ruminations on things his professors said were going to happen, could not come true if he did not let them. He saw that he had the power to determine the eventual outcome, despite what they were throwing in his path.

The next morning he had his wife bring him some photographs of his earlier graduations. There was one which he liked more than the others. It captured him with a broad smile on his face, wearing his cap and gown, standing with diploma in hand in front of his car at the time. It prompted him to recall the happiness and confidence of former times, and he knew he could attain all that again, and he would. All he needed to do was "update" the picture.

Taking a pair of scissors, Wally O. cut out the image of himself, removing himself from the background of his old car. He pasted the clipping to a new piece of paper and added a graphic border. He proceeded to cut the words "mind over matters" out of a magazine and appended them to his "goal-vision."

Whenever he felt the fears and the insecurities creeping into his mind, Wally O. would reach for his picture. He would force himself to think of his chosen destination, instead of the potholes along the route. He maintained his thoughts on his goal—his master's degree. He visualized himself at graduation, holding the diploma, as though it were an accomplished fact. He lived the vision, feeling the success and satisfaction of having proven his professors and detractors wrong; and most importantly, he savored the exhilaration of having overcome all his "mental demons."

Wally O.'s recovery progressed rapidly. Upon his release from the psychiatric ward, he re-entered his master's program. True to his commitment, he practiced solid mind management. He stayed focused on his ultimate dream of graduation. He fought his way through the negativity and the doubts of his "mentors" on the faculty; and he prevailed.

In May of 1991, Wally O. graduated with a master's degree in design from the College of Architecture and Interior Design of Arizona State University. He was the only one of the six originally accepted into the program to make it.

Just before graduation, he sent out resumes to 10 respected universities, seeking a faculty position. He received an offer from one of the more prestigious institutions in his field, and accepted it. Wally O. now lives in the Midwest, a very productive, happy Assistant Professor of Art and Design.

Wally O. says:

> Mind management makes you or breaks you. Fear is a choice. I learned that. I learned to choose not to be afraid. You can fight fear, and you can beat it. I think everybody has to go through that, one way or another. We all have to learn to live our life and not let other people tell us what to think of ourselves.

POINT OF CONFIRMATION

Before leaving this subject, I want to stress one point. Some treatment for depression relies solely on medication, and I firmly disagree with that approach. Without mind management counseling, there exists little hope for eventual cure. Such approaches foster dependency, and patients seldom progress back to independence. Medication must be viewed as supportive and palliative, not curative.

Yet, it is also truth, that in dour states of depression, the abyss can be too deep for the patient to scale alone. Without stabilizing medication, effective mind management for them is not feasible. Once they are stabilized through medical support, then they can deal with the source of their anxieties.

People I have interviewed, who have overcome severe clinical depression, reported an abiding feeling underlying the whole experience. They sensed, deep down, even in their darkest moments, that they were not their blues, and that they could rise above them, if they could obtain competent assistance. They sought the help, and they succeeded. That tells me that even in those dark states, the mind senses both the source and the solution to the dilemmas.

Human beings have emotions, but we are not our emotions. We have bodies, but we are not our bodies. How we feel and what we feel do not determine our course unless we choose to allow that.

You might not be able to choose all the events in life, or what others do or say, but you certainly *do choose* how you will react to them. Your thoughts allow you to rise above the turmoil.

Again, the over-arching message of this book: You make the choices. You choose your thoughts. You choose your attitudes and responses. The biggest factor in what happens to you is how and what you think—something over which you have total control.

CHAPTER 8

Above Your Age,
Above Your Aches

Your age and your aches get in the way of achievement only because you allow them to. Age and aches are not the ultimate limiters, they are not the cause.

"If people would just realize what they can accomplish by simply setting a goal and then taking one step at a time," said blond-haired, blue-eyed Pat Cohan, a woman who sat in one of my recent seminars, looking properly refined and dignified.

She recounted to me the first time that she decided to do "something crazy" as she describes it. Pat had taken a guided excursion by train down into Mexico. Her intended destination was Copper Canyon, bearing some resemblance to Arizona's Grand Canyon. En route, at one of the train stops, Pat saw a group of Tarahumara Indians.

All my life I had been fascinated by National Geographic and articles about native cultures and primitive tribes. When I actually saw these people, some spark inside me ignited: I just loved them. I don't know how else to say it; I just fell in love with these people. I was fascinated, and I wanted to learn more about them.

Pat almost missed her train, she was so absorbed taking pictures and trying to communicate with these people.

The "end of the line" was a small town called Creel, a lumber town. Pat learned that a number of Tarahumaran Indians lived in the vicinity. They made a little money by cutting lumber in the mountains and bringing it down to Creel to be sold. The tour stayed in Creel for two days, during which time, Pat's fascination and interest in the Indians grew. She could hardly tear herself away as the tour pulled out of town and headed back to the United States.

When Pat Cohan returned home, she immersed herself in books and articles about the Tarahumara Indians. At length she decided:

> I wanted to go and see a primitive tribe; I wanted to find and observe these people for myself. But, I thought, "How can I do that? I don't want to just go on a safe, supervised tour. I want to go to see them living, how ever they live. But I don't have any way."

As her desire to accomplish this goal grew, Pat formulated a plan. During her brief time in Creel, she had met a family which traded with the Tarahumara Indian. She reasoned that if she took another tour back to this place called Creel, and then got off the tour, perhaps she could convince this family to let her stay with them. And if they would, then maybe she could get enough information to be able to go up into the mountains and find a Tarahumaran village.

This rudimentary, very tenuous, plan stayed with her. Often Pat would have bouts with legitimate doubts and questions. She describes waking up in the middle of the night, thinking:

> Who are you? What do you think you're doing? You must be crazy—you're pushing 50 years old. You're going to take off all by yourself down to Mexico. You speak only a little bit of Spanish, and no Tarahumaran. You don't know

anything; you're nobody; you're not an anthropologist; you've never studied...How could you do this? You must be crazy.

Driven by something she really wanted, she didn't give up. Pat battled back with herself. There was no good reason for why she wanted to do this, other than she just wanted to do it, and she decided that was good enough, and nothing was going to stand in her way.

So she paid her money and took the tour again. When she got to Creel she left the group. She convinced the family she had met to let her stay with them. Then, like a ravenous investigative reporter, Pat began asking questions of everyone in Creel, showing them her pictures of the Tarahumaran Indians. Finally she learned that a postman went twice a week back into the primitive parts of the country to a place called Batopilas, which, she learned, was the closest "town" to where the Indians lived. Pat got the postman to agree to take her along.

While in Creel she met an anthropologist who, along with a travelling companion, was there to study the Creel area. The anthropologist was so impressed with Pat's determination, she requested permission to travel along to also find the Tarahumarans.

They rode in the back of a pickup truck to Batopilas. Pat then started interrogating everyone in Batopilas. Nobody knew anything. No one could help. Undaunted, she just kept asking questions. Eventually, Pat ran into another anthropologist who, together with his travelling companion, also decided to follow Pat on her quest.

She chuckles as she relates the irony of the scene—a 50-year-old woman with no formal training, leading two bona fide anthropologists and their companions into the wilderness of Mexico.

All I had going for me was love and desire. It was just
something I was determined to do, and nothing was going
to stop me.

Following one lead after another, the party travelled
deeper and deeper into primitive country and eventually located
a family of Tarahumarans living in the backlands of nowhere.

The anthropologists settled down some distance from the
Indians. They said, "If you're a real anthropologist, you do not
disrupt the culture. You observe it from a distance."

Pat was undaunted:

I said, "That's not why I came here. I came to meet them,
to know them, to get close to them." So I took my supplies
and marched over to the Indians and started talking to them,
using sign language and clumsy gestures.

One woman knew a little bit of Spanish and, with that
small advantage, Pat could communicate fairly well with her.
This Indian woman was grinding corn, and Pat sat down and persuaded the woman to teach her how to grind corn and other such
chores. They became friends.

Pat spent several days with the Tarahumaran Indians. As
the friendship with this one particular woman grew, they discussed their families. The Indian woman became rather puzzled
at one point. When she learned that Pat was the mother of three
children, she asked, "How is it possible that you could have
raised three children and not know how to grind corn?"

Pat says:

To me, my whole trip was worth that one moment—that one
communication. I still cherish the realization that in so
many ways this woman and I were very much the same, and
yet so far distant as far as our cultures were concerned.

Pat has gone on to achieve an array of remarkable goals
subsequent to her expedition to the Tarahumaran village. Part of
what makes her story so remarkable centers on the fact that at

one point in her life she was not in very good health.

She was involved in a car accident which had virtually crippled her. That was followed by three pulmonary emboli, and she nearly died. Some of her doctors doubted she would walk again, but she had learned to get around. Even so, she thought of herself as a debilitated person. Speaking of this period in her life, she said:

> I had accepted the fact that I was going to be sort of an invalid for the rest of my life. I felt I had to reconcile myself to that because I was in such bad condition that my doctors could not even give me a stress test. They did not think my heart could handle it.

In her weak condition, incapable of vigorous exercise, Pat was susceptible to other illnesses. She contracted hepatitis and that problem led to several other complications. She had developed a severe heart condition with high blood pressure, and was in frank pain most of the time. Her whole physiology was "out of whack" and Pat was growing more infirm by the day. The shelf in her bathroom looked like a pharmacy. She was taking numerous medications, feeling weak and eventually began to sense that she was dying.

Pat had seen this happen to others. One health problem begins unravelling the whole physical fabric. As one system fails, it adds burden to other systems, which in turn begin to malfunction. Before long, like tumbling dominoes, the systems become so hard-pressed, debilitated and fouled-up, the person dies. Pat sensed that she had commenced this process and was progressing directly to her demise.

> After that experience, I decided I could do whatever I put my mind to. I could do anything, if I really wanted to do it. And I decided that I could do something about my failing health. I made a choice: I was going to stop dying and live.

Pat Cohan chose life! In an impressive way. Foremost, she has regained her health. She began to take charge of her body. Commencing with small increments, she began to exercise and follow sound principles of nutrition. Pat noticed tangible improvements, small at first, but unmistakable nonetheless. Step by step, she grew stronger, and she got her life back.

Her increased energy, strength and self-esteem led to a reawakening. A broad vista of possibilities opened up to her view, and, once again she began setting and reaching other impressive goals.

As I mention some of her notable achievements, I urge you to keep visualizing Pat Cohan. Picture a refined, well-educated woman in her mid-50s—the kind you see chairing civic committees, leading social organizations in your community, and promoting the symphony. This elegant, poised, woman has, in her fifth decade, climbed to the base camp on Mt. Everest, has set the U.S. national record in her division in the bench press, and has backpacked for ten months across China, Nepal, and India, winning awards for her National Geographic-style photographs.

> You have to want to do something. You have to believe that something is possible and, once you believe it's possible, it is. You can do just about anything, no matter how difficult.
>
> I climbed to the base camp on Mt. Everest on the Tibetan side. I saw these gigantic climbs in front of me and thought, "There is no way. How can I do this?" Then I would push that thought away and say, "I'm going to do it because I know I can take one step," and I'd take that one step. Then I'd take three breaths and I'd take the next "one step."
>
> No matter how steep or difficult it got, I just kept that same frame of mind. And taking one step at a time, I reached my goal. There are not many 50-year-old ladies who have climbed to that base camp. [17,500 feet.]
>
> I learned a great lesson on that quest: As long as you can take one step, you can go anywhere. You can do anything as long as you take it one step at a time.

Pat believes that virtually anything is possible if people are willing to take one step, and then another, and then another, and not give up.

> If I can do it, anybody can. There really is no reason they can't because we are all the same. It's all in whether or not you are going to believe in yourself. You have to have the faith that the goal is possible, and then it is. I can even move a mountain one tablespoon at a time. You know, you really can.

Her power-lifting achievement is a testimonial to the same exhilarating principle.

> I have some physical limits—I have a bad back, I have a bad shoulder and hip, but I have sort of strengthened all the muscles around all my problems. And I have done so much more than I ever thought I could.
>
> That is why I liked the bench press; the problem with my back and hip weren't involved if I was lying down on the bench. So I could just concentrate my efforts on a part of me that didn't have too many problems.
>
> When I lifted a certain weight, I just kept wanting to do more. I kept saying, "If I can do this much, maybe I can do five pounds more." And I found I could.

One day Pat was discussing goals with her personal trainer, Leon Peterson. Leon told Pat she had progressed to the point that she could start competing. She said, "Oh, that can't be possible."

Leon and Doug Grant, founder of Nutri-Strength, (Doug is also a world champion in his division in the dead lift and bench press), looked up the record in the women's master's division (age 40 and over), and Pat realized she wasn't that far away from the record. She was thrilled. "I had never won anything in my life before," she said, "And I decided to go for it." Laughing, she mentions that she did win the "dead-man's float" contest in grade school because she was overweight and therefore quite buoyant.

It was pretty exciting and wonderful. When I realized, at my age, at 57, all of a sudden I'm competing in an athletic event, and I have the possibility of winning, I couldn't wipe the grin off my face. I kept thinking, "My gosh, this is me; I'm an old lady. No, I'm not an old lady. Look at me, I'm an athlete."

When I set the national record I could hardly believe it. For a sedentary old woman it feels pretty good. I have all these trophies on my mantle now, and my children are thrilled.

Pat smiles and shakes her head as she recounts her discoveries and her accomplishments. Sometimes she just lets her pleasant laugh punctuate the conversation. The delight she takes in life seems like a school girl's, and her eyes kind of sparkle as she says:

I kept myself from a lot of things in my life, because I believed I couldn't do them. Now I believe I can do anything. Do you know what I am going to do now? I'm going to go skiing!

CHAPTER 9

Above Your Troubles, Above Your Trials

You are not your body, your blues, your age or your aches. Neither are you your troubles or your trials. Whenever I think of people accomplishing great things despite great trials, I think of Terry Fox. And, whenever I think of Terry Fox, I am inspired to be better.

Terrance Stanley Fox, a curly-headed student at Simon Fraser University, was diagnosed with an aggressive form of cancer, osteogenic sarcoma. Osteogenic sarcoma is a virulent, fast-spreading malignancy which starts in the bone. It breaks out of the boney capsule early, hideously and rapidly invading the rest of the body. Often, even before the victim realizes he or she is tired, let alone sick, the cancer has spread to vital organs like the lungs. Even today with our best medical modalities, the survival rate for osteogenic sarcoma is pitifully low.

At age 19, Terry received the dread news. The pain in his right leg was caused by cancer. Terry was informed that he would need to undergo radical surgery. Surgeons were going to remove his leg as far away from the cancer as they could without taking his life. He would receive an artificial leg "to get by on," a shaft of metal and plastic with a mechanical hinge at the knee.

Terry was told that aggressive follow-up treatment, radiation and chemotherapy, would follow. Gruesome side effects were enumerated. Anyone who has been close to such a regimen can legitimately question whether it is all worth it. Sometimes the morbidity of "the cure" seems worse than the mortality of the disease.

As the reality of his situation sank in, Terry explored options in his mind. He knew he could feel sorry for himself. No one would blame him, if he did. Languishing in the clinics and hospitals of Canada, he knew he could plunge into the depths of self-pity. He could become bitter. He could grow angry and acrid, upset with God, resentful of the world, furious with the unfairness of it all. He'd have every right. He was only 19—his whole life was in front of him—and now he was facing the very real prospect of pending death.

There was, however, something else that Terry knew: Anger or self-pity were choices. No one could force those responses upon him. Terry saw that either of those two avenues held consequences that would only increase the damage the disease would do to his life. He chose neither. Terry Fox decided that for whatever time he had left, it was time to live!

He underwent the amputation of his right leg. Chemotherapy followed. Fighting back, he learned to use the artificial limb. He walked; and then he learned to run. Terry then announced to the world that he had set a goal: He was going to run what he titled "The Marathon of Hope." The Marathon of Hope was a prodigious goal.

Marathon was hardly the word. In track and field, a marathon has come to mean 26.2 miles. Terry dedicated himself to running the entire breadth of his native land. The vast country of Canada, from the eastern boundary of Newfoundland to the western boundary of British Columbia, spans a distance of over 5200 miles.

On a dreary April morning, Terry Fox dipped an aluminum toe into the Atlantic Ocean, turned west and he started to run. Every day he ran, day after day.

Most of us are impressed when someone will train for months to run a marathon, and we understand when it takes days afterward to recover. Think of that, and then think of the kind of drive, commitment and stamina Terry Fox had to muster in order to run a marathon *every day*. Rain, hail or shine, he ran. Days turned into weeks; weeks turned into months. On he ran.

Finally, 3339 miles into his goal, the disease caught up with Terry Fox. The Marathon of Hope ended just outside of Thunder Bay, Ontario as the cancer had spread to his lungs. He died a few months later just short of his 23rd birthday.

Thunder Bay is built on the cliffs which form part of the northwestern boundary of Lake Superior. If you ever get a chance to go to Thunder Bay, don't you dare miss going to the Terry Fox Memorial. It will move you deeply. People stand there in quiet reverence, before a shrine to the valiance of the human spirit. Many leave flowers, some shed tears.

The memorial is constructed of native Canadian rock, a stone bridge arching from one pedestal to another. Fittingly, it symbolizes the interconnecting power of Terry's goal, linking Newfoundland with British Columbia and uniting all the hearts in between. Fixed on the face of the arch, there are the chevrons of the provinces and territories of Canada. Atop the bridge is a bronze statue of a 21-year-old amputee in a running posture, a mechanical device for a leg. Whenever I picture that monument in my mind, I hear the words of Terry Fox in my ears:

> I learned that you can find the energy. I learned that you can find the resources. I learned that your mind can amaze your body, if you just keep telling yourself, "I can do this; and I'm going to do this."

Take a look at the people you admire. Are they people who have had something handed to them? No, they are women and men who have passed through fiery tests, met adversity and overcome it. Their lives testify that none of us are robots with preset programs. Neither are we victims of circumstance unless we think we are. No one is predetermined; we are free. You are the programmer, not the program!

THE FORGING OF HEROIC QUALITIES

For all he did, Terry Fox has become a legend. Rightly so. Everyone in Canada knows his name and knows his achievement. His fame has spread to other countries. He has become an inspiration to thousands of people he never knew existed. Yet it is the whole story which teaches the full gamut of lessons.

Glory does not come easily. You have to opt for the upward trail not the course of least resistance. This is a rule with no exceptions. Terry Fox was not spared the price just because he had cancer. The now-revered Canadian hero was hundreds of miles into his goal before his mission gained much attention. That's what impresses me *most* about him.

When Terry Fox came up with his idea, despite its nobility, the world paid no notice. When Terry announced that he wanted to raise huge sums of money for cancer research, no one opened their checkbooks. Cheering crowds did not line the office of Blair MacKenzie, executive director of the local Cancer Society, as Terry came to offer his all. From MacKenzie himself, the response was less than a standing ovation. "We get a lot of requests that are a little off-center," he said. Dismissing Terry as a crack-pot, Mackenzie merely said, "Fine, organize it yourself." And Terry did.

Even the greatest intentions must be converted into the evidence—the evidence of action—before people will pay attention. Perhaps it is even an eternal law of the universe: No one will bother to believe in you, until you have proven your faith in yourself.

Only a few people saw Terry Fox off on his Marathon of Hope. At first, he was virtually alone. Hardly anyone took notice. Along the first hundred miles there were no adoring crowds cheering encouragement. During the next hundred miles, there are no throngs to assist him when his clumsy, artificial leg kept coming off, throwing Terry to the pavement. The masses were not there to offer encouragement when the cysts and blisters emerged, burst and bled. He had to keep going, encouraging himself, moving on, mile after mile, in anonymity.

For a while, it seemed no one would comprehend what this curly-headed hop-runner was about. At an early press conference Terry remarked, "Nobody knew what we were talking about."

Respect for Terry came sparingly, grudgingly. He seemed to earn it, one stride at a time, as he jarred himself over the first thousand miles of highway.

The road was rough in more ways than one. He was nearly hit by rude motorists; run off the road by truckers; and police, labeling him a traffic hazard, would not allow him onto the Trans-Canada Highway. Terry, however, remained committed. He had not expected it to be easy, even though his goal of raising money for the defeat of cancer was a "motherhood" that anyone should have readily embraced.

Eventually, his unwavering commitment triumphed over the inattention and apathy. Word of Terry's undaunting courage spread. Hearts were touched and wallets were opened. Money started rolling in, and the Marathon of Hope began to realize its objective.

Running across Ontario, his goal reached "critical mass" and the explosion finally occurred. A swarm of 10,000 admiring people thronged city hall when he pounded his way, doggedly, through the streets of Toronto. National, then international, television coverage caught the vision and heralded the message.

Terry lived to see the fund-raising aspect of his dream fulfilled. Before he died, he knew that he had raised $2 million for the Canadian Cancer Society, more money than any other person in its 42-year history. I am glad he lived to see that. It would have been nice for him to have known that the fund went well beyond that to reach over $20 million.

Terry Fox rose above his illness, above his pain and above his knowledge that there was not much future in front of him. Even the very knowledge that he was dying did not diminish his living.

MORE THAN THE MONEY

We never know how far the efforts of one human being can reach. Terry himself said:

I just wish people would realize that anything is possible if you try...dreams are made if people try.

The legacy of Terry Fox is that we all can succeed. We all have the power. The mind and will, when faithfully applied, conquer mountains. We can climb them, even move them.

Terry faced an insurmountable Everest, but he made no excuses. He did not blame fate or society. He did not curse the heavens or the powers that uphold them. He accepted responsibility for what his life would be, in spite of the disease and impending death. He, like all of us, was put to the test by the adversities in his life. He was the victim of a cruel disease, but he did not wilt; he rose above it and went on.

I never met Terry Fox, never shook his hand. I was one of the oblivious masses, who did not hear of him until he was gone. Yet he has had a positive impact on my life. I would also venture to say that he has had a significant impact on the lives of people who have been through my seminars, for I often recount his saga.

Frequently when I am in the midst of telling his story, I see people in the class start to weep. Sometimes, although I have told it hundreds of times, I do too. We do not weep out of pity, and not for his pain. We do not weep that he died. We weep out of admiration for someone who had the courage to rise above fear, rise above troubles and trials, dream big and, despite the odds, dig down and go for it. And, most of all, we weep because we know, down deep, that we long to do that too.

SECTION III

EXERTING CAUSE ON THE CAUSE

When you control causes, you control effects;
and **you have power.**

WE ALTER OUT DESTINY BY ALTERING OUR THOUGHTS.

CHAPTER 10

Laws of the Mind (1 & 2)

We long, like Pat Cohan, Terry Fox, Renee Riddle and others, to rise above our circumstances and current levels of achievement. And, yet, many of us do little more than wish. Changing the wish into reality requires exerting cause on the cause. Since it all comes down to mind management, it is not only logical, but necessary to understand the fundamental laws on which the mind operates. Socrates said:

> If I understand "why" a thing should be done, then I can move heaven and earth to do it.

Once we recognize the premises and parameters of mind function, we can develop solid strategies to improve behavior and performance.

The laws of the mind are not complex, but their ramifications are enormous.

LAW NO. 1: MIND MUST THINK

The first obvious characteristic of the human mind is its constant state of activity. You can guide your mind, but you cannot stop it. The activity of the mind-brain complex is non-stop, virtually synonymous with life itself.

More than a decade ago, the legal and medical professions locked horns, grappling with the definitions of life and death. Landmark cases, such as the Karen Quinlan case, debated the question, "What constitutes life, and when is someone actually dead?" The answers did not come down to hearts, lungs, corneas nor kidneys. It all came down to mental activity.

When the brain waves go flat, life has ended. Mental activity is the cardinal sign of life! When that ceases, hearts, lungs, corneas and kidneys can then be removed and transplanted to another individual whose brain still operates. All other organs are interchangeable. Life is synonymous with "the presence" of mind.

Life and thought are inseparably related. Mark Twain wrote:

> What a wee little part of a person's life are his acts and his words! His real life is led in his head, and is known to none but himself. All day long, the mill of his brain is grinding, and his thoughts, not those other things, are his history. These are his life, and they are not written, and cannot be written...Biographies are but the clothes and buttons of the man—the biography of the man himself cannot be written.

Truly, the record of our life is none other than the transcript of our thinking, and our true biography is the story of our ever-flowing thoughts. The mind must think. You can guide it, but you cannot halt it.

RAMIFICATIONS OF LAW NO. 1

One of the basic tenets of life, the Law of the Harvest, states: "As you sow, so shall ye reap." Nowhere does this principle hold more true than in the garden of the human mind. Your thoughts are the seeds of your actions.

Since your mind is in a constant state of activity, the planting process and the corresponding harvesting are always going on. You are continually generating a never-ending flow of causes, producing an endless yield of effects.

If you take a passive approach to mind management, it does not stop the planting *or the harvesting.* It simply means you take your chances on your outcomes. When you do not actively manage your mind, you allow the world around you to largely dictate your agendas. If you're unselective with your thoughts—you do not stop the "harvests"—you merely leave them up to chance. You relinquish control.

On the other hand, each of us possesses the supernal ability to appraise our thoughts. We can think about what we are thinking, right in the process of thinking it. We can change topics, in a flash, any time we want, moving from something inferior to something better, if we prefer. No thought is forced upon our mind, we choose each and every one of them.

We can select which seeds get planted in our mental garden. By exercising that prerogative wisely, we wield tremendous control over what happens inside us and outside us. Choosing positive, constructive thoughts, while rejecting negative, destructive or unproductive thoughts, yields the consistent fruits of success, satisfaction and joy.

One final observation: The fact that your mind must think also means that you are always in the game! There are no spectators in the game of life. None of us gets to sit on the bench and spectate. Like it or not, you and I are constantly in the game. We're playing the game right now.

You have chosen to use this time to read, to provoke yourself to think about something worthwhile. I commend you for that. As you continue to fill you mind with productive thoughts, your choices will unavoidably bear good fruit. The consequences of your mind management are irrevocable. They are ongoing and inescapable.

LAW NO. 2: MIND THINKS BOUNDLESSLY

The second Law of the Mind is: Mind thinks Boundlessly. Not only is the mind in a constant state of activity, it is virtually boundless in its capabilities. Let me highlight only two of the numberless ways your mind thinks boundlessly.

First, you have imagination and creative ability without limit. You can think of anything. Dreams and imagination are unlimited.

Don't pass over that prerogative too lightly. Think of what a marvelous power you possess to dream, invent and create at will. There are no inherent ceilings or boundaries. You can turn knowledge and perceptions upside down. You can take facts, information and data and mold them into ingenious new meanings and purposes.

One simple example of this common occurrence is seen in our ability to play on words and develop multiple meanings. When I write the word "liver" you probably think of the organ in your body tucked under your rib cage. And, if I were to suggest that a person has a problem with his or her liver, you would think of something like hepatitis. Yet, you could look at the word in a new way, and define a "liver" as one who lives—a lover is one who loves, a liver is one who lives. Carrying this word play further (and thus, giving it more "life"), you could say: Some people have trouble with their *liver*. The force inside them, "the liver," is not active and enthusiastic. The "liver" inside is not eager to embrace, experience and make the most of life.

Obviously, word play is just one minor facet of the mind's creative, innovative abilities. Every experience, every fact, every impulse is a potential catalyst which can trigger some marvelous new outcome or result.

Sifting and selecting, keeping or discarding, your mind moves through incredible volumes of input every waking hour. At any given moment you have the ability to construct new combinations of thoughts. You can assemble commonplace facts into stunningly clever associations, breaking through into new territory. You can entertain anything from the whimsical to the technical, from the mundane to the spiritual.

Thinking in new ways is a challenge for all of us. It may not be easy, but it is definitely possible. The free-flowing river of thoughts takes the course of least resistance, but only because we permit that to occur.

Environment, culture and education all play crucial roles in forming a framework for our thoughts; and often we allow this framework to become quite rigid. However, our frameworks have been acquired along the way; and, since they are acquired, they are also subject to transformation or replacement.

The mind will go to work, if we direct it, and make miraculous ascents to new heights. The boundaries, borders or prisons are not inherent. You *can* think boundlessly.

ANOTHER SENSE

A second sense in which your mind thinks boundlessly is that it is **ungovernable by any other force.** No one or no thing can bind your mind and make you think thoughts that you don't wish to think or choose attitudes that you don't wish to select. Each one of us is absolutely independent in that internal sphere. No external force, no other entity, can dictate your thought processes.

Over the years, people have wondered about one person's ability to control another's thoughts. The consensus among authorities is, it doesn't happen. In most instances of "brain washing," the instigators so torture the body or humiliate the personality that the person will represent a submission to external ideas in order to get out of the painful episodes.

But, even that proves the point. The individual must submit, must acquiesce; and without that internal permission, no outside idea can be imposed. Nothing external can mandate that submission. The individual has to yield or consent. No external force can decree thought.

Each one of us is uniquely independent in that internal realm. You, and you alone, have the power to choose what you think. Only you choose your moods, your attitudes and your disposition at any given moment. Ultimately, you choose, through your thoughts, the kind of person you become.

This truth was driven home to me when I read *Man's Search for Meaning* by Dr. Viktor Frankl. (A book of great merit, I highly recommend it.)

Frankl was an Austrian Jew, a psychiatrist by profession, respected in his field. During World War II, like so many Jews, Frankl was incarcerated in the concentration camp Auschwitz.

In that brutal environment, as he was going through that indignant ordeal, he observed human actions and reactions. He experienced it all himself, and assessed how others responded as well. Frankl came to some piercing insights.

Paraphrasing him, he said:

> The Nazis took away every piece of property. They even took the clothes off our bodies, the fillings out of our teeth. They took away every human right, except one. The one thing the Nazis could not take away from us was our ability to think freely; and each one of us, [and here comes the key word], *chose* for ourself what we would become in the midst of this ugly, atrocity-filled environment.

Frankl observed that some people chose to return kindness and charity. It did not matter what was inflicted upon them. They chose to forgive and refused to hate back. Many people managed to stay upbeat and positive most of the time. Such people expected to survive, and, he said, those people tended to survive.

Others, not surprisingly, became angry, bitter and full of hatred. Some gave up. Sometimes, in quite formal ways, people relinquished their hope in the future. Frankl described this as a pivotal moment. The day they abandoned hope, and decided things were never going to get better, was the day they began to deteriorate mentally, spiritually and physically. It was as though, he said, they had signed their own death certificate. Some almost immediately took to their cots, pulled their knees up into the fetal position, and, within a matter of hours, would be dead.

Frankl's conclusion needs to be read and pondered. He said:

> Everything can be taken from man but one thing: the last of the human freedoms—to chose one's attitude in any given set of circumstances, to chose one's own way. In the final analysis, it becomes clear that the sort of person the prisoner became was the result of an inner decision and not the result of camp influence alone.

Contemplate the phrase—"was the result of an inner decision"—for a minute. In the end it was not the Nazis, not the fences and barbed wire, not the atrocious external circumstances which dictated the person's life or character. It was his or her inner decisions. Each one of the prisoners chose—*chose*—how they would deal with the forces around them. Each person's life became a reflection of those inner decisions.

I hope that thought will empower you with greater resolve to take charge of your inner game.

Frankl continues:

> Fundamentally therefore, any man can, even under such cir-cumstances, decide what shall become of him—mentally and spiritually.

I want to comment on that last word. Frankl is not saying that he believes that mankind saves itself spiritually. He is saying, if a person takes on spiritual qualities and traits, it is because they choose to acquire them. By their attitudes and through their thoughts, they determine what qualities become woven into the fabric of their character.

Correspondingly, and just as easily, a human mind can wall itself off from any attribute that it chooses.

TO COWER, TO COPE OR TO CONQUER

We have all seen people that, for whatever reason, have chosen some of the more negative attributes and have decided to mope through life. You see it in their body language; they sort of slump around. When they speak, there is a noticeable whine in their tone.

Similarly, we also know individuals who have decided that they are going to angrily storm through life, flailing and lashing out at people along the way. They engage in an on-going fit of temper. You actually feel them walk into the work place, emanating some glowering spirit. Slamming their purse or briefcase down on the desk, they let the rest of us know they have arrived, and we had better stand our ground. When you meet somebody like that and say, "Have a nice day," you really put the pressure on them.

These souls have made a decision. They have decided, of their own free will and choice, that they are not going to have a nice day (and we can't make them). That, you see, is precisely and exactly the point. They've chosen. It's not the collisions, the obstructions, the frustrations out there that have determined the outcomes. It's their internal choices. They have decided to be angry and irritable today.

On the other hand, we all know people who really have had some hard knocks in life. They have gone through some things that a human being should not have to endure; but, you would never know it by talking to them. They are warm and up-beat. They broadcast a positive, attractive force. They're fun to be around.

When you see somebody like that, don't you dare blame that on astrology, or the tides of the sea or the phases of the moon. Those people have *decided* that they are going to be problem-solving, challenge-surmounting people.

Abraham Lincoln summed it up perfectly:

> It has been my observation that people are about as happy in life as they make up their minds to be.

I am no Lincoln, but in my experience I have come to the very same conclusion. People are about as happy and about as successful in life as they really choose to be.

Who cannot be touched and inspired by the strength manifest in these words of Helen Keller?:

> I seldom think of my limitations, and they *never* make me sad.

Happiness is not something you buy or find. It is something that, despite the vicissitudes of life, you decide to *be*.

Here, then, lies the crux: You cannot stop your mind, but you can control it...And *only* you can control it.

Responsibility cannot be shifted to anyone else. It rests precisely on the shoulders of old "number one." Successful people do not shirk responsibility, they accept it. They quit making excuses, and they depart Non-responsibility Land. They get out of the blame-fixing business. They *own* their own outcomes. Much greater progress can be made when results become diagnostic tools instead of judgments about our capabilities.

Dr. Norman Vincent Peale believed that even our spiritual progress rests on individual responsibility and initiative:

> When by **a conscious act of will** one turns his mind to God, fixing his thought upon the divine source of power and energy; then in such manner as if he had turned a switch... spiritual power begins to pass into him.

OH, YOU MAKE ME SO MAD!

Just because I'm writing a book on mind management does not (unfortunately) mean I have completely mastered the subject. (And I even have an advantage over you; I get to attend a seminar on this stuff about three times a week.)

My wife and I are raising a family. If you have raised a toddler or two, you know that you don't exactly have to be Sherlock Holmes to find your house out of order. You also know you don't have to be a Smurf to talk yourself blue in the face, trying to get your rules across to these little people.

I am the kind of father that has a Moses complex. I like to come down from the mountain with laws to give to the children in the valley to obey. One of the laws in the Deaton household is called The First Law of Messes. Most people assume The First Law of Messes to be, "If you make it, you clean it up." That, friend, is the *Second* Law of Messes. The First Law states, "If you don't make a mess, you don't have one to clean up." (Thought of that one all by myself.)

We have The First Law of Messes plastered on the walls of the Deaton home. We have preached endless sermons on the same. The message should be clear.

However, it appears to be the ultimate goal of the children in Deaton Valley to break this commandment and irritate Moses. At least that seems to be my mental state as I come home from work after a hard day. Hear the rationalization coming already? What does it matter that I have had a hard day? Well, it helps my rationalization. (Do you have your violin tucked under your chin?) Poor Dennis: It was a hard day at work.

Returning home, I walk into the living room. A six-year-old has perpetrated some disaster there. Now Dad walks up to confront Child. (Dad will fix Child's self-image for about two decades, right?!) "Look at this mess!" As the tone and pace crescendo, Dad amplifies, "Don't you know the first law of messes: 'If you don't make one you don't have one to clean up?'

Are you *ever* going to get that into your head? Child, you make me so mad!"

"You make me mad," comes reverberating off the living room walls. Freeze frame here for a moment and analyze, please. Here you have a supposedly mature adult who has just said to a six-year-old that the child has the diabolical, mystical power to bind the adult's mind and *make* him mad.

Do you buy that explanation? I imagine not; and you are right. It's a cop-out. But if it isn't Child's fault, there is only one other choice in the room. Dad.

As I am into my tirade, this idea of taking responsibility for oneself flashes into my mind. I am convicted by my own words. Getting hold of myself, I apologize. Among many things, I conclude by saying, "Above all else, Child, I want you to know that you don't make me mad."

Obviously, when really analyzed, we all see it. No one in this whole city, county, or state can bind Dennis Deaton's mind and make him mad. Only Dennis "makes" Dennis mad. The sooner he comes to that realization, the better off he's going to be.

The confrontations of life which happen "out there" do not have a hard wire connection to what happens "in here." There is a critical junction and separation. What happens externally is what happens externally. What happens *internally* amounts to a decision. The sooner we admit that, the sooner we put ourselves on the road to mature growth and faster learning curves.

Albert Schweitzer said it pretty well:

> Man must cease attributing his problems to his environment, and learn again to exercise his will—his personal responsibility in the realm of faith and morals.

CHAPTER 11

Laws of the Mind (3 & 4)

In the previous chapter, we discussed the first two laws of the mind: Mind Must Think and Mind Thinks Boundlessly. With that groundwork we address two more laws of mind function.

LAW NO. 3: MIND THINKS EXCLUSIVELY

The third laws states that mind thinks exclusively, one thought at a time. It doesn't matter how busy you are, how great the demands, or how high your IQ, your conscious mind can only focus and concentrate on one thought at any given moment. Scientists call this property lateral or peripheral inhibition.

Although your mind can flit from idea to idea at such blazing rates of speed that sometimes you have the impression you are entertaining simultaneous thoughts, such is not the case. Your conscious mind maintains an exclusive stage. Only one player can perform there at any one moment, and you have absolute control over which player it is.

Any thought that dwells on center stage, any thought which becomes dominant in your mind, represents a choice, a selection, a preference on your part. Choose it well. Thoughts that dwell on center stage are directives to the body to be brought into working reality. You are a goal-achievement mechanism of the highest order. Every dominant thought urges you, actually propels you, to fulfill or complete it.

At one time I thought of this trait as an unfortunate limitation. "Wouldn't it be wonderful," I mused, "if I could focus on multiple topics at the same time. I could talk on the phone, balance my checkbook, write a book and read a book all at the same time." Think of it, on Saturdays, you could work and relax simultaneously.

The more I consider that, however, the more I appreciate what a marvelous advantage this offers us. If we stop being so passive about mind management, take control of our thoughts—become more selective about what we dwell on—we can virtually ensure consistent positive outcomes. Furthermore, we have a great antidote to cure much that ails this society.

Fear, worry, and doubt cannot exist in the same mind with confidence and faith. They have to be exchanged for one another. If you are plagued with fear, worry, and doubt—if anxiety is always lurking over your shoulder—it is because you are not managing your mind. You are allowing your imagination to be exercised in its negative format.

If you ask yourself, "What could go wrong?" your mind will answer that question. Your imagination will conjure up any number of unattractive scenarios in response. (In brainstorming and problem-solving sessions, that question may be productive. However, most of the time, we use it as a lever of discouragement.) For some of us, one trip through the imagined disaster is not enough. We know we can do better (at making it worse), and the mind goes on to picture an even greater catastrophe.

I know this from personal experience. I used to be a world-class worrier. If there had ever been Olympic games in worrying, I would have easily been the gold medalist; I could out-worry anyone. I'd have, on a fairly regular basis, my 3:15 a.m., "SuperBurruba," Dennis-Deaton-crash-and-burn experience. You may have had one or two of your own. At 3:15 in the morning, you wake up, body rested, mind alert. You wonder, "Why am I not sleeping?...Something must be wrong." Dread creeps into the room like an eerie fog. You go back and relive every bad experience you ever had—failures, klutzy mistakes, arguments you had with people years ago. You put yourself right back in the scene. Formulating a sharp retort, you say to yourself, "Oh, I wish I would have said that to him, that would have really gotten him."

Then you think of your bills. You contemplate the recession. Maybe your business will fail...maybe you are going to get laid off...the national debt will destroy your future. Soon you are picturing starving people in the streets...you and your children are among them...they look like refugees from Somalia. And on it goes. For an hour and a half, you toss and turn, tying the sheets in knots and your stomach as well.

I have come to validate, at least to my own satisfaction, that such experiences are totally self-permitted. You don't have to put yourself through them; and I don't any longer. When you feel those negative players moving onto center stage, formally and adamantly refuse to entertain them. Shift your thoughts. Put your attention on better subjects.

One of my "safety valves" is to ask myself, "Dennis, what do you *want* to make happen? What would you *like to see* take place in the next six months? Where do you want to be with your business, where do you want to be with your family, where do your want to be temporally and spiritually?" Constructing a picture of where I want to be in six months—what I want to make happen—does not allow me to wallow in negative experiences of the past.

The one thing your mind has no power to do is to alter the past. Too many of us spend precious time, ruing, fretting and regretting things that can no longer be changed.

Life is a face-forward opportunity. It is up to you to make the most of it. Stop letting the trash of the past clutter the gardens of the present and the future. Throw it out; stop ruminating!

Returning, over and over again, to events of the past makes a two-fold error. First, you re-inflict on yourself the pain of that previous experience. (This is literal, by the way.) Your body reacts to those mental movies as though they were the actual experiences.

Second, because you allow them to dwell on center stage, those negative visions reinfect current behavior. Thoughts beget action. That is the power of dominant thought. The phrase "self-fulfilling prophecy" is not a figure of speech, it is a literal phenomenon. Ironically, all this ruing and regretting reintroduces the very things we ought to abandon.

Often, many of the things we keep reliving are actually quite trivial in nature. Yet, by focusing on them, we turn them into major stumbling blocks. On the other hand, major improvements happen, immediately, the moment you cast them away and cease allowing them to homestead on center stage.

LAW NO. 4: MIND DRIVES BODY

Body is a dependent entity, a functionary of the mind. Body, with brain as its governing organ, does nothing independent of mind. Mind wills; brain directs; body enacts.

Every feat, every action, every conscious movement is initiated by mind, and the brain-body complex responds with fairly accurate obedience. The body may be viewed as a servant of the mind to bring ideas into physical reality. Mind is independent, brain-body is dependent.

Granted, a great synergism exists between mind and body. Physical weakness and incapacity of the brain-body complex affect mind, but mind has the greater role and exerts the greater effect. A principle of direct reciprocity governs this relationship. When mind operates positively and constructively, body benefits. Body, under such influence, becomes stronger, more efficient and even more resistant to disease. Balanced, homeostatic harmony results among the systems of the brain-body complex. In such a state, body then returns the favor, and reciprocates benefits back to mind. The body, working at its best, facilitates the powers of the mind. You think better—more clearly, vigorously and productively.

The reverse also holds true. When we dwell on the negative, we create a downward spiral. Pessimistic states of mind adversely affect the physiology of the body. Justly, the body returns these goods in kind. Lower energy levels, greater susceptibility to disease are well-documented consequences of negative thinking. In turn, the mind's powers diminish when the brain-body complex is impaired.

In this classic interdependent relationship, body affects the mind and mind affects body, but mind takes precedence. Body's effect on mind underweighs mind's effects on body. Mind is sovereign, body is servant.

SOMETIMES HE CRIES

When the mind commits, the body has no choice but to respond. The body may resist or complain, but in the final analysis, mind rules.

Davis Phinney, a world-class cyclist and former Olympian, won, over the course of his career, nearly every major bicycle event in North America. Internationally, he has also proven himself, winning stages in the Tour De France on at least two occasions. One of his reflections underscores the point:

> After training hard, your body reaches a different plateau and it's a neat state to be in. You get to the edge of physical breakdown, of totally blowing out, then you recover and go on. The key is to cut off your body from the neck down.

There are times when you think you can't turn the pedals anymore, but you know just ahead you'll get a little break. It does get bad sometimes. I mean, I cry a lot during races...but I keep hustling because I know I'll feel better in a while.

Body solicits, but mind decides. Mind needs to listen to body, and exercise wisdom and judgment. Masochistic or careless destruction of the body is not being advocated here. Pain and fatigue need to be respected, but they do not govern human outcomes. Human will rules. When you decide to press on and overcome, despite the pain, your body must obey. The ability to bring body into obedient compliance to noble vision constitutes greatness.

KATHLEEN THE GREAT

A journalist once asked conductor Bruno Walter to cite his greatest experience in music. "To have known Kathleen Ferrier and Gustav Mahler, in that order!" was his reply. Kathleen Mary Ferrier lived forty-one and a half years, a brief but remarkable life. She went from being an unknown telephone operator in Blackburn, England, to one of the greatest contraltos of the 20th century. Few singers have gained greater respect and admiration.

Kathleen did not start out with her eyes on a singing career. She grew up playing the piano and was proficient enough to accompany some of the notable singers of the time. She did not picture herself a virtuosa, but others who heard her voice were impressed, and they encouraged her. Finally, at age 22, she began taking voice lessons, and her gift developed rapidly. Over the next 18 years, she sky-rocketed to international prominence and thrilled audiences with her great talent.

Tragically, in her prime she was stricken with cancer. As the disease progressed, Kathleen heroically continued her career.

Cancer is insidious. At times people stricken with it think they are winning, only to have their hopes cruelly dashed by recurrence of the monster. Kathleen battled through the highs and lows, maintaining a demanding professional schedule. Eventually it became apparent that the disease was going to prevail.

Many people were anxious to have this marvelous voice recorded before it would become silent. Kathleen herself had long desired to collaborate with the great Bruno Walter in recording some of Mahler's works. Accordingly, arrangements were made to combine these two great talents and preserve the moment for generations to come. The objective was to record three arias of Mahler. The first two went well, but there was trouble with the third, "Um Mitternacht," which was the most demanding of all.

Only those who have experienced severe and extended illness can appreciate the weakness, the debility, the pain. Only they can understand the effort it takes to just dress oneself and move about. Only they can comprehend what superhuman effort would be required to perform at one's optimum in such a condition.

Kathleen Ferrier had endured several operations and weeks of extended radium treatments which ultimately proved futile. The combined ravages of the disease and the treatments had left her physically decimated. The bones in her body were weak and brittle. During one of her final performances, her left leg splintered as she turned on it. Yet, amazingly, she courageously completed her performance that night.

The audio technology at this time (the early '50s) was cumbersome and awkward. Recording sessions back then were ponderous experiences. Kathleen endured many interruptions and retakes. All this while she was sick from the disease, weakened from the treatments and exhausted from the physical and mental battles she had been waging. Naturally, there was the additional pressure of rising to her optimum level. She knew this would be her legacy, and generations to come would judge her by this recording.

"Um Mitternacht" concludes with a grand crescendo at the end. It requires great strength, control and concerted power from the soloist. This final segment was giving the technical crew fits. For two hours they struggled to achieve the proper balance between Kathleen's voice and the orchestra.

On each attempt Kathleen had to summon all that energy and all that strength in order to deliver the performance everyone had hoped for. She had no way of knowing whether this was to be the performance which would outlive her or not. Attempt after attempt went for naught. By the time the technical bugs were eliminated, Kathleen was weak, exhausted and hurting. Those present feared that the whole agonizing experience was going to end in failure and disappointment.

The technicians, Bruno Walter, the orchestra, and Kathleen gave it another heroic try, but neither Bruno nor Kathleen were satisfied with it. The next attempt had to be scrapped also because Kathleen's voice cracked during the crescendo. The director called for a break to let Kathleen rest, and she limped weakly to a chair.

After a few minutes, it was decided to give the recording one more try. As Kathleen rose from her chair, she faltered, twisted her back sharply, and crashed to the floor. There was a sickening silence in the studio. Everyone thought it was over. Kathleen looked up and saw the concern and the disappointment on all the faces. And then, (mind drives body, you know) she picked herself up, dragged herself to the microphone, and sang "Um Mitternacht" as it has never been sung before or since. Bruno Walter had tears running down his cheeks, but his beat did not falter. The take was an artistic and technical masterpiece.

Every goal, every deed, every act—heroic or menial— begins with an idea. When any fleeting thought becomes a center of attention—a dominant thought—the body faithfully responds. The physical body is the servant, an awesome and articulate instrument, that brings focused thoughts into the physical world. In the final analysis, **behavior is mind driving body in fulfillment of dominant thought.**

.

CHAPTER 12

Dominant Thought Management

No matter what field you care to name—music, scholarship or business—success or failure hinges on DOMINANT THOUGHT MANAGEMENT.

According to the laws of mind function, mind thinks exclusively, one thought at a time. Those exclusive thoughts drive body. Especially does this hold true with the ideas we habitually dwell on. The attitudes we automatically rehearse, the mental programs we play and replay, the scenarios we revisit in our idle moments—these frequent themes on center stage—these are our dominant thoughts; and they are incredibly potent. They determine the routes and destinations of our lives. BEHAVIOR IS MIND DRIVING BODY IN FULFILLMENT OF **DOMINANT** THOUGHT.

BY THEIR FRUITS YE SHALL KNOW THEM

Jesus of Nazareth plainly taught this concept. His concise summation, "By their fruits, ye shall know them," speaks libraries on the subject. Clearly, he indicated that you could tell what was going on inside a person by what showed up in their behavior. The dominant thoughts of the mind cannot be hidden. They continually and unerringly reflect themselves in our words and in our actions.

Want to read people like a book? Learn to really listen to their words. Listen to what they say and how they phrase it. A two-minute conversation will reveal volumes. Dominant thoughts will sound through loud and clear. With practice, you will be able to discern, in a matter of minutes, what people think of themselves, their basic philosophies, and how they approach life.

For example, if "life is difficult" forms their basic premise, you will have no trouble hearing it. Simply ask them, "How is life for you these days?" and, three sentences into their response, you will hear references to recent past trials and indications that they expect more to show up shortly. (And, by the way, take a wild guess as to what *will* show up for them in the near future.)

If "I love life; and it's full and rewarding," forms their foundation, you will have no trouble discerning that either. Their conversation will reference recent experiences which have brought joy and delight. Excitement about the future will be evident—they expect more happiness, more goodness. (And, correspondingly, guess what will show up for them in the future?)

Words and behavior reflect perfectly what goes on in the mind. Ask someone, "How do you look at money?" It will not take long to detect their dominant thoughts about finances. "Money is hard to come by;" "Money is a tool I use to get things done;" "Say what you want, the bottom line in life is cash;" "Money is the root of all evil." Whatever that person thinks about money will soon become clear in their expressions. The software determines what shows up on the screen.

Furthermore, to test the accuracy of your diagnosis, simply look at their financial fruits. All the evidence will be plainly manifest. Those who see money as a useful tool to benefit themselves and bless the lives of others, will have money. Those who believe money is hard to come by (and "probably a tool of the devil, anyway") will be living hand-to-mouth.

I repeat what is vital to remember: Life is a creation. And you create it in your thoughts. What you allow to become dominant in your mind, not only drives your body, it creates your world.

I hope you will ponder this concept. You now have in your possession the most powerful diagnostic tool for self-analysis and for self-improvement in the universe.

Want to read *yourself* like a book? The self-same principle applies. By your own fruits, you may surely know yourself and your own dominant thoughts. If you are pleased with the fruit appearing on your trees, you know the root cause; and, by all means, continue your course. If the reverse be true, you know the source and what you can do to improve the harvest: Alter the thoughts you are dwelling on.

You might think that it is absurd for me to suggest that we *don't* know our own habitual thoughts, that we are not aware of what dominates our minds. But, I am going to stand my ground and say, "It's true! We don't."

One of the hardest things we do is to see ourselves and to recognize what we are generating in our internal world. And it will remain forever difficult until we accept that the world we experience—that which shows up all around us—how the world treats us—is the creation of our own minds. When we accept that, we then have a way to diagnose ourselves. Life plays our dominant thoughts back for us.

Not happy with your career? Not happy with your monetary life? Not happy in your relationship with your partner? Guess what you are seeing? The fruits of your own mental habits. Change them.

Love your career? Enjoy going to work each day? Happy with your relationship with your son or daughter? Take heart in your feat, and acknowledge yourself. Those are creations of the positive, productive, dominant thoughts you have generated. You are reaping the pleasing harvest of the good seeds you have sown.

Your power to change and continually beautify your world becomes more direct and more rapid as you exercise your self-diagnostic power. Immense value lives in this: **"By *your* fruits, ye shall know *yourself.*"**

And this is not even the beginning. The dramatic impact you can have on your own life is but a prelude to the possibilities. You can move beyond that to exert influence on the gross elements outside yourself. Self-improvement, as vast and marvelous as it may be, is barely the beginning of the value and benefits that flow from effective dominant thought management.

FOR THUS THE UNIVERSE WAS WROUGHT

As I have already proclaimed, we do not comprehend, even slightly, our potential power. That which can be accomplished through concentrated singleness of purpose and focused mental effort (dominant thought management) falls so far beyond our expectations and comprehension that it defies classification or description.

In chapter three, "The Matter of Thought," I shared Henry Van Dyke's statement:

> We build our future, thought by thought,
> For good or ill, yet know it not.
> Yet, so the universe was wrought.

This statement is but the reiteration of inspired declarations throughout the ages. Isaiah records, "The Lord of hosts hath sworn, saying, 'Surely as I have thought, so shall it come to pass: and as I have purposed, so shall it stand.'" Linking that idea with the account of the creation in Genesis, we see that Judeo-Christian writings affirm that God created the universe. And he did it by the exact principles we are describing in this book. When the elements were assembled and worlds came rolling into existence, God was not manning a shovel somewhere. He was exercising the supreme powers of his own mind, and the action was "mental" not physical. In short, the heavens and the earth were created *in, by and through* the singular, fortified state of mind, which in some sectors is called "faith." Even to call this "an awesome force with incredible power" is to utter the most egregious understatement in history.

If you take the word, faith, out of religious contexts entirely, the world is full of evidence that the resolute state of mind *does* produce miracles. The numerous stories of victorious women and men which I have shared in this book are but a minuscule roster of miraculous accomplishments wrought by focused human beings. Helen Keller observed:

> Reinforced with faith, the weakest mortal is mightier than disaster.

In summary, whether you apply it to religious or metaphysical contexts, or just to the boundaries of life itself, the ability of the mind to enter a state of strength which produces remarkable results needs to be noted and respected. Beyond that, it needs to be sought for and developed, for it is your loftiest power and highest capability.

SEQUENTIAL STEPS

We all possess this power in varying degrees of refinement. Whether you call it "mental toughness," "complete confidence," or "faith," it still comes down to a state of mind. Greatness, mediocrity or total ineffectiveness are all states of mind, the results of varying degrees of mind management. When we perfect our abilities, really master our minds, we possess the power "to move mountains."

And (shout for joy!) effective mind management is something which can be developed and perfected by each one of us. In this quest, **first things come first**. In human development one grand principle presides: Certain things precede and prepare the way for others.

Human progress unfurls as a grand sequential process. Each correct principle we master brings an array of benefits and gains. And, most importantly, the lesser leads to the greater, each principle bringing higher benefits and powers. My grandfather, in his accurate, colloquial wisdom, used to say, "Doing hard things makes it easier to do something harder."

Like a grand stairway, each truth leads to the next. This sequence of continuous improvement stretches before each one of us. Infinite in scope, there are no upper bounds. Thus, what matters isn't your place on the stairway as much as your direction and the consistency of your progress.

For progression to be strong and continuous, the sequence must be respected. Caterpillars cannot become butterflies by circumventing the chrysalis. Certain things must, and do, precede others. We crawl before we stand; we stand before we walk; we walk before we run; and we run before we high jump.

Sometimes without knowing it, we thwart ourselves by getting out of sequence. We attempt to high jump before we have mastered balanced walking. When that happens, we become frustrated and get down on ourselves. We must understand that the problem is not in our overall potential, merely in our sequencing. We forget that the power of higher principles comes from mastering preparatory steps.

How many times have you witnessed the wisdom of the "return to the basics" strategy? When high performers are "out of synch" and floundering, they get back "in synch," and excel again when they revisit and reestablish their prerequisite skills. You cannot have power in the higher when you lack power in the lower.

Wisdom dictates that we exert care to learn and master the foundation principles. Each step contributes strength and has an essential purpose. Certain things must precede others; preparation precedes power.

Napoleon Hill, in one of his most significant and inspired statements, declared:

FAITH IS A ROYAL VISITOR WHICH ENTERS ONLY THE MIND THAT HAS BEEN PROPERLY PREPARED FOR IT; THE MIND THAT HAS BEEN SET IN ORDER THROUGH SELF-DISCIPLINE.

IN ONE WORD

To slice right to the core of preparation, the biggest single need, in one word, is **DISCIPLINE**.

What comes to your mind now that I've used the "D" word? Many people hold negative connotations. People get hung up on it. Ask a teenager what the word "discipline" means and you'll hear the response, "Punishment." Even adults, who expand their definition somewhat, retain undertones of stoicism and anguish. Discipline need not be synonymous with pain.

The Latin root actually signifies "learning in an organized way." Learning brings joy. Growth and improvement stand as the most exhilarating and pleasant experiences of life. Discipline enhances and accelerates that process, providing access to happiness.

A friend of mine recently saw this concept in action at a local ice-skating rink. As she paid for admission, she figured she would soon be gracefully floating around the rink. Dorothy Hamill and Nancy Kerrigan make it look so easy, you know. Not only was she unable to do any fancy turns or jumps, she could barely move without pratfalling. After numerous gaffes and blunders, she clearly saw (and, several parts of her body felt) her lack of skill. Her lack of disciplined learning proffered no skill, which, ironically, was a confinement (a sort of "punishment").

As with most subjects, the truth about discipline is just the opposite of what many of us think. Discipline is not punishment, the lack of discipline is. Undisciplined action does not bring joy, mastering correct principles does.

A second-rate piano player once remarked, "Patti is such a great pianist, I would give anything to be able to play like she does." The truth is the poor player had started piano lessons about the same time Patti did. Her idle statement is self-indicting. Despite what she said, she declined to discipline herself to practice the hour a day for six years like Patti had.

For Patti, the discipline—dedicated learning in an organized way—led to the ability to sit down and play at will, even composing selections of her own. Discipline led to freedom, satisfaction and joy.

Discipline proffers direct and proportionate returns. The greater the degree of self-discipline, the greater the powers and prerogatives. Benefits accrue all along the way, the rewards getting ever greater as you progress. No gain is inconsequential. Every step adds.

Effective mind management and discipline are inseparable. In the grand sequential process, these preparations lead to a state of mental strength which can ultimately harness the energy and elements of the universe. Discipline breeds faith.

CHAPTER 13

Eliminate Mental Clutter

We cultivate discipline and prepare our minds for even greater works when we learn to handle one of the great plagues of our generation—MENTAL CLUTTER. We have so many tasks, obligations and responsibilities to manage these days, our minds become infested with the "I-have-to's," the "I've-got-to-remember's," and the "I-can't-forget-to-do's." All this administrivia clogs our creative conduits like plaque in hypertensive arteries. This mental sclerosis damages and weakens us just as surely as any physical disease.

As with arterial disease, the obstructions of our creative vessels relate to diet. We often feed our minds a diet of junk food and let it hang around, clinging to our attention, congesting and choking off the flow of higher levels of thought.

THE HIGH PRICE OF CLUTTER

Most of us try to carry too much on center stage. Much of what clutters our mind is of a menial nature. Grocery lists, tasks, reminders and a vast spectrum of inconsequentia compete for our attention.

Many of us will go to our graves with our novels unwritten and our symphonies uncomposed, because we allowed routine chores to dominate our attention and occlude our creative arteries.

Trivial daily tasks proliferate, precluding focus on greater projects and priorities. Yes, we get stamps on our letters, get the envelopes into the mail boxes. Yes, we follow up on all our meetings, answer our voice mail and leave our messages. But is that productivity?

I present a lot of seminars to large corporations, many of which are reducing the size of their work force. Cutting costs, they seek more productivity from fewer workers. Human beings **do** have the capacity to take on more responsibility, but only with the proper training and tools. If you load them up without imparting the skills to manage more detail, you shut down the creative output. If you impair innovation, the long-term picture turns bleak. The short-term savings may be illusory.

I raise the issue, not to counter restructuring, but only to fix on the real objective. Greater productivity at lower costs calls for *sharpening* the creative edge.

Those of you who are in the work force realize the need to get more done and not get mired in the routine. The answer comes down to mind management. You get trapped by the menial if you only think about the menial.

Eliminate the mental clutter. Organize your mind by using a comprehensive, daily self-management system.

SIMPLIFY YOUR SYSTEM

In the process of creation, the mind must be *supplied* with detail, not *occupied* with it. You need a daily system which will support your mind, not encumber it.

Most of us have sensed this need for a support system. We, with best of intentions, have assembled an array of

instruments to jot down notes and reminders; to track commitments, appointments and tasks; to project, calendar and plan.
The intent is fine, the method is flawed.

The problem with most systems lies in segmentation and
fragmentation. We use too many tools. We have assembled an
array of multiple instruments which separate and gravitate to far-
flung locations. Consequently, we find ourselves looking for the
stuff that helps us manage the other stuff.

We use a conglomeration of calendars, note pads, little
black address books, purses, wallets, planners, phone-fax direc-
tories, little yellow Post-its, the backs of envelopes, lists, engineering pads, palm-tops, lap-tops, files, folders and
shredders...all of which are stuffed in bulging briefcases, purses
and satchels. Can we really call this proliferated, scattered
menagerie "an organization system" and keep a straight face?

This collage creates some distinct disadvantages. Studies
show that the average white-collar worker in North America
spends 51 minutes a day *looking for* routine items of daily trans-
action and/or routine information, such as addresses, phone
numbers and phone notes. Some consultants would jump all
over that statistic. Calculating what everybody in a given
company made in 51 minutes and, coming up with some gar-
gantuan figure, they would try to horrify upper-level management with how much money was going down the drain.

Yet, that would be only a paltry quantification of what is
really perishing. Those 51 minutes represent but the tip of the
iceberg. Those interspersed speed bumps on the thinking
highway disrupt focus, break concentration, interrupt continuity,
thrash attention spans, introduce frustration and diminish the
greatest resource the company has, the mind power of its people.

Progress has always (and only) been a function of our
creative capacity. With the barrage of data, deluge of communi-
cations and avalanche of knowledge overwhelming the mind, the
need for control becomes even more acute. Studies show the
quantity of available information in the world doubles every 600

days. Success in the future will be exclusively synonymous with mental fitness. Those who can think clearly amid the chaos will prosper.

If you're getting the drift and want to do something about organizing yourself and eliminating mental clutter, here are three valuable habits to cultivate for a workable self-management system:

1. CREATE A PORTABLE OFFICE

Create for yourself a "portable office." Not planner, *office*. Many people have designated a landfill for some of their stuff (a planner), but their mind is still littered. Think in more *comprehensive* terms than merely a place to jot appointments and phone numbers. You need something which is transportable, but complete enough to allow you to manage *life*.

Don't compartmentalize, thinking, "I have a professional life; I have a social life; I have a personal life." What you have is life; and, you have one mind that has to manage the whole project. Your mind does not work location-specific. When you're *on* the job, things flash into your mind regarding outside concerns. When you're *off* the job, things hit you about your career. You need something at your fingertips to allow you to respond to the whole spectrum.

You thwart planning and creative thinking when you have to postpone decisions and conclusions for lack of key information. "When I get to the office, I'll look that up and decide," is counterproductive. Get the essentials organized. Put them at your fingertips and get rid of the speed bumps. You'll be markedly more productive when you cut the delays and make more decisions on the spot. Stop deferring.

I have designed a portable office for myself and others, which has worked marvels for me. It is a multi-faceted planner, journal, task manager, appointment log, directory, long-range calendar, goal monitor and multiple reference tool in one comprehensive, easy-to-use format. Smaller than a thin attache case, my organizer goes with me everywhere. The system I use is called the TimeMax Organizer.

My portable office functions as an able administrative assistant. The details of each of the multiple projects I manage are easily accessed behind a dedicated tab in my organizer. I have a way of registering tasks and commitments so that they come back to me, automatically. When a thought worth noting hits my mind, it goes in the journal section on a dated day page. The information and notes can be retrieved at virtually any time, wherever I am, in a matter of seconds.

Above all else, use a system that assists you to identify and stay focused on genuine priorities. My organizer reaffirms my current, proximate, highest priority on a daily basis. Grandfather spoke a pearl of wisdom: "Never get caught up in the thick of thin things." I encourage you to take his advice. Seek to be priority driven, not contingency driven. A good self-management system should accomplish that for you.

2. CONSOLIDATE

Incorporate as many tools into your office as you possibly can, and get rid of the scattered collection. Eliminate all redundant sources and resources. Condense and consolidate. If you don't have to explore so many galaxies (and go where no man has gone before) to get a phone number, you not only save time but more of your daily transactions become instinctive.

With a consolidated directory, for example, whenever you need a phone number, fax number or address, you don't have to ponder possibilities. You won't have to think, "Is that in the Rolodex at the office, on Uranus-6, or on the refrigerator at home?"

You do have a refrigerator, right? Most normal Americans do, and they turn them into minor shrines. When I walk into somebody's home and find that I have made their "fridge" list, I count it as a tremendous compliment. (People only put their nearest and dearest on their refrigerators.) Some people think my organizer is a bit large, but they use a *refrigerator* for a calendaring device.

You can turn much of the menial over to habit when you have a place for everything, keep everything in its place, and that place is always the same place. Use only one set of calendars; one directory; one project management system. Have only one place for notes; only one place for reminders; only one place for appointments. By deleting redundant sources, you simplify the explorations. With only one alternative, your referencing becomes automatic—literally a "no-brainer."

3. HAVE THE OFFICE WITH YOU WHEREVER YOU GO

Create for yourself a portable office, consolidate as many tools into it as possible, and then use it. Take it with you. Not just for your profession, remember the purpose of your comprehensive office is to help you manage *life*—the whole spectrum. An inclusive system can become the most valuable assistant, sometimes at some of the most unexpected moments, but only if you have ready access to it. Create it and carry it.

BOTH MEANS AND ENDS

Never lose sight of the *real* purpose of the office. It supports the mind, not the other way around. Use your organizer to retain everyday detail so your mind does not have to. Get beyond task lists, agendas and notes. Use your mind to create achievements, not to maintain and manage the status quo.

Great creative potential can become lost in the infra-structure of life. Beware the high price of mental clutter! Clutter steals. With more stealth than the most artful cat burglar, clutter sneaks onto center stage and takes over. Don't get lost in the routine maintenance activities of life. There is an enormous difference between being mentally busy and really thinking.

Organization pays. And the benefits go way beyond daily productivity. The beauty lies in the development of mental order and discipline, while divesting yourself of menial cares. As you create more order, you take great strides upward to higher levels of mental performance.

CHAPTER 14

Sustain Concentration

With the clutter out of the way, you can bolster your personal effectiveness in other ways. You can really hone your ability to focus and concentrate. Greatness is more a matter of mental focus than raw physical skill. World champion hurdler, Edwin Moses, said, "Concentration is why some athletes are better than others."

The ability to set worthy objectives and really focus—not wander off into la-la land—proves to be the crucial skill which lifts us above mediocrity and sets our higher mental powers in motion. Voltaire said, "No problem can withstand the assault of sustained thinking."

ATTEND TO YOUR ATTENTION SPAN

Our times, as no era before us, demand mental effectiveness. Elevated competition in an ever-expanding global market, and the resultant mergers, down-sizing and new ways of doing business, place increased demands upon us. The mind must process and assess information, form value judgments, and make accurate decisions at faster rates. At the same time, there exists more potential distraction and interruption than ever before. It is easy, in our times, to mistake mental busyness for real thinking.

Although the ability to concentrate has never been more necessary or valuable, signs indicate that forces pull us in the opposite direction. Studies indicate that people of our grandparents' generation had longer attention spans than we do. Rather than expanding, ours are shrinking.

Among the culprits contributing to this decline lurks television. It's not just the insipid subject matter of the programs, the formatting is a concern. So-called entertainment or educational segments are shortened while the advertising segments expand. Then, even the advertising segments are aggressively subdivided into short, glitzy splashes. When was the last time you saw a 60-second commercial? Advertisers tell clients not to waste money on 60-second spots. Audiences won't pay attention that long. The norm has been 30-second blurbs, but lately the trend has moved to 15-seconds and even to what they call "7s." They pitch one simple message, loaded with sensory-rich hype, and then move quickly to another product before the mental circuits overload.

The programs, too, seldom rise above mental mush. If there was ever bubble gum for the mind, it is "American Gladiators." Have you seen this program? If "lack-of-redeeming-value" were a hole, this would be the Grand Canyon. They even named it wrong. "Steroids On Parade" would have been more accurate. On October 22, 1991, the Los Angeles Times ran an article which caught me totally off guard; it implied that there were a *number of great things* about "American Gladiators." (I didn't think there were any.) Mark DiCamillo, spokesperson for the producers, stated:

> One of the great things about "American Gladiators" is it is
> a sport for the '90s, designed for the American mentality
> and television audiences! All the events on the show are 60
> seconds or less. It's perfectly planned for the kind of
> attention span Americans now have.

Reluctantly, we must admit, the man has a point. Rather than becoming stronger mentally, we may be becoming mental midgets. (I should have said, vertically challenged.)

Possibly, you have detected some symptoms, but you may have discounted them. Do you have a little difficulty getting started, or staying focused, on a project which requires creativity and detailed thought? When you read, do you fade in and out of concentration? Do you have to go back and reread pages because your mind has wandered from the topic? When you pray, do your thoughts stray onto mundane tasks at home or at the office? Do trivialities like, "Did I leave the iron on?" or "Is the garage door closed?" deflect your communication? Such mental lapses seem small and innocuous. They annoy us a bit, but we dismiss them as no big deal. Be careful.

VANQUISH VACILLATION

Unmanaged thoughts, like water, take the course of least resistance. But they do so only with our permission. We allow ourselves to vacillate back and forth between two poles, positive one moment, negative the next.

This ambivalent state is the norm for many human beings. Very few pessimists are so single-minded that they never contemplate a glimmer of hope, howsoever brief. Unfortunately, the opposite is also true. Even the most positive of us have not consistently eliminated the negative. While we have the innate capability to obliterate doubts, most of us spend a lot of time vacillating between the two sides. And, in that wavering, we lose strength.

After announcing a universal promise to all people, "If any of ye lack wisdom, let him ask of God," James advises us:

> But let him ask in faith, nothing wavering. For he that wavereth is like a wave of the sea, driven with the wind and tossed. For let not that man think that he shall receive any thing of the Lord. A double-minded man is unstable in all his ways.

No answers or rewards are promised to those who waver. And where does such vacillation occur? What is the source of the ambivalence? One place and one place only—our own minds.

Vacillation is self-inflicted. It amounts to a state of mind which we can control. Unquenchable optimism can be learned. Those of us who want to be more single-minded in the positive should emphasize attention to our attention spans. The ability to concentrate on desired results—to stay focused on positive goals—to not allow our minds to tear down what we are trying to build up—grows out of awareness and effort. Exercise builds muscle.

NOT BORN WITH IT

A few years ago, settling in for a six- to seven-hour flight from New York to Milan, I took my assigned seat on the aisle. A distinguished looking gentleman with an erudite manner took the aisle seat on the opposite side one row in front of me. I thought when I saw him, "This man looks like a college professor."

With him being seated in my range of vision, I could not help but observe him. As the flight attendants reviewed the safety instructions (all the stuff about oxygen masks with bags that don't inflate) he took out of his briefcase a *very* thick book. It appeared to be new. He opened the cover carefully and creased sections of the pages.

Again, I emphasize the thickness of the book, it made *War and Peace* look like TV Guide. He began to read. I thought, "He must be going to Europe for three months, if he plans to finish that book."

Soon we were in flight. The captain turned off the seat belt light; we were free to move around the cabin (like there's all this room to romp and play, right?). This gentleman continued to read. I couldn't help watching him out of the corner of my eye. Bam, a page turned. Bam, another.

Before long, headphones were offered, they planned to show us a movie for the intellectually-challenged (Bamby, the Vampire Slayer). This man didn't flinch, falter, grimace, jerk or shiver; he just kept reading and, bam, the pages kept turning.

The attendants served peanuts and soft drinks, and then meals. The reader kept right on reading. He only paused long enough for lunch and a couple of short stretch breaks. I flipped through the airline magazine; he read his book. I took a nap; he read his book. I walked up to the front a few times to see if the captain was still on board; he read his book.

Sitting there, in the midst of all these distractions and potential deflections, his concentration did not waver. He stayed focused.

By the time we were descending into Milan, he was finishing the final pages. Closing the book, he replaced it in his briefcase. By now, I was so impressed with this man's concentration span, I could not stand it any longer.

I leaned forward in my seat, reached out and tugged his sleeve. As he looked around, I said, "Who *are* you?" (That is my favorite line from "The Princess Bride"—Inigo Montoya asking the Dread Pirate Roberts, "Who *are* you?") Rather than speaking, he handed me a business card. Sure enough, true to my first impression, he actually was a professor at a northeastern university. We exchanged greetings.

Then I said to him, "I'm so impressed with your ability to concentrate. I noticed you devoured that huge book, and hardly took your eyes off of it. You have an incredible attention span."

He replied, "Why? Can't you stay focused on one subject for eight or nine hours at a stint?"

Before I could say, "Well I sat through 'The Ten Commandments' without dozing much," he asked, "What do you do for a living?" I just couldn't bring myself to tell him that I teach mind management.

My point is simple: The professor was not born with that notable attention span. He developed it. He, through dedication and regular study hours, acquired the capacity to stay on one topic for great lengths of time. You and I can do likewise.

To develop concentration I recommend a daily reading session. If you will hold a **daily** "study hour," **at the same time each day**, you will notice significant improvement within just two weeks. With each successive session, you will focus more rapidly, become less distractable and concentrate more deeply. Moreover, you will remember and retain more.

A daily reading hour is the easiest and most beneficial method for stretching your attention span. For other ideas on enhancing this quality, read *Brain Building* by Marilyn vos Savant, an excellent book with practical guidelines for "exercising yourself smarter."

The key, according to Ms. vos Savant, is consistency:

> Just as the human body can be strengthened and toned to muscular power through body building exercise, so too the mind can be strengthened and sharpened. You can't build a great body in a few hours; the same goes for your intellect. Remember that the secret to the success of any exercise program is repetition, repetition, repetition. Only then will you begin to see results.

THE CONFESSIONS OF GENIUS

Increasing your attention span opens the way to genius thinking. Read the autobiographies and journals of geniuses; they will tell you that themselves. **Geniuses do not claim to have exceptional brainpower**. They consistently deny possessing vastly superior mental hardware or being innately more intelligent than other people. Such expressions are not just excessive modesty. They are sincere. Geniuses, universally, do not perceive themselves to be extraordinary. They know themselves, and they recognize, in the genuine core of their being, that they are not super-human. What they *do* acknowledge is that they have certainly *learned to think*. They reveal that the mental edge they enjoy lies in knowing *how to concentrate their intellect and discipline their minds*.

We have all heard Thomas Edison's self-effacing statement, "Genius is 99 percent perspiration; one percent inspiration." We have heard it so often, in fact, that the meaning has evaporated. We hear the words, but they no longer convey much meaning.

Hear it again, geniuses are telling us they have no inborn advantage. Providence has not arbitrarily bestowed greater intellect on them and capriciously withheld it from the rest of us. There are laws upon which all results and benefits are predicated. Creative, insightful people have applied those laws. They have controlled the conditions of genius and have reaped the rewards. And, you can do it, too.

VISION: BY-PRODUCT OF CONCENTRATION

VISION IS SYNTHESIZED! Stunning innovations, piercing insights, genius ideas—the creative output of the mind—result from a process bearing striking resemblance to what chemists call synthesis.

**SYNTHESIS: the combining of separate substances or
          elements to form a new coherent whole.**

Almost all of us have had some formal exposure to chemistry. In chemistry labs, students learn an important truth: They can produce new substances by exerting control over seemingly spontaneous, "uncontrollable" events.

In the final analysis, the combining of elements into a new substance is a spontaneous occurrence. In that dramatic moment when energy changes state and a new substance is formed, things happen which are outside the direct control of the chemist. What takes place is truly, as the term says, a *reaction*.

Yet chemists do have control. The chemist can decide when and where that spontaneous event will occur by *taking control of the conditions.*

In chemistry *conditions* are critical. Some reactions demand very precise requirements with low tolerances for deviation. Criteria are so precise and delicate that even slight variances will not yield the results. Yet, with absolutely no exception, every time those given conditions are meticulously fulfilled, the reaction occurs.

All this is analogous to the human mind and what takes place in the creative process. Vision and innovations are synthesized. The bursting of a new idea into your conscious mind occurs spontaneously. Some catalyst suddenly triggers a bolt of insight. Eureka! Enlightenment! You see something you have never seen before. This new vision results from mental synthesis. Discrete concepts have been combined into a new coherent whole.

The spontaneous nature of that familiar event has led many of us to conclude that we have no control over that marvelous process. That conclusion is erroneous. We do have control. In the same sense that a chemist controls a chemical reaction—by controlling the conditions—you can govern your creative process.

The creative mechanisms of the mind, working wonders all about us, constitute the fountainheads of progress. Our standard of living and our circumstances are by-products of mental creation. Yet few bother to analyze how the process works.

You can direct your creative genius. You can not only select the topics and subjects it works on, but you even have a lot to say about *when* those ideas come. The techniques for doing this are what I call the "Technology of Innovation." This technology centers in DOMINANT THOUGHT MANAGEMENT.

Vision *is* synthesized. Vision—breakthrough insights, great ideas—results "spontaneously" when certain controllable conditions are met. You exert intelligent control over creation through controlling your dominant thoughts.

CONDITION: MENTAL EFFORT AND FOCUS

Edison alluded to a significant condition. Clearly, Thomas Alva Edison was a creative dynamo, a genius. He was considered by many the greatest inventor in history. With only three months of formal education, he patented 1093 inventions and improved numerous others. People tend to explain his achievements (and excuse themselves) by calling his output "a gift."

Edison, himself, does not let us off that easily. He says that his contributions resulted from hard work, rather than from some mental gift. Perspiration, quantitatively, far outweighed inspiration.

Note carefully, Edison is not denying or minimizing inspiration, and neither am I. He is actually identifying one of the requisites to receive inspiration.

Both components are indispensable. Yet one precedes and precipitates the other. Perspiration alone is not sufficient. Without the inspiration, there is no genius. Yet inspiration does not arrive unsolicited either. Edison points out the crucial condition needed to obtain the breakthrough: Mental effort. Focus. Concentration. Sustained thinking.

Inspiration and vision are available to all, irrespective of education or background. Whoever applies the law and adheres to the conditions, gets the result. And the converse holds true, no one who cuts the corners receives the reward. The laws of the universe are just.

A SECOND WITNESS

Thomas Edison is not the only genius who testifies of this principle. Note the similar explanation of genius offered by Alexander Hamilton:

> Men give me credit for genius. All the genius I have lies in this: When I have a subject in hand, I study it profoundly. Day and night it is before me. I explore it in all its bearing. My mind becomes pervaded with it. Then the effort which I made the people are pleased to call the fruit of genius. It is the fruit of labor and thought.

Here is genius explaining genius. He is saying it comes down to dominant thought management. Innovation and insight come as a result of focused concentration, the fruit of labor and thought.

Real breakthroughs are seldom a re-invention of an entire subject. In most cases, they are an addition to the accumulated wisdom of other thinkers and amount to the next logical step forward. When one mind gains a comprehensive grasp of the existing territory, ponders awhile, it can deduce where all that information is leading. Suddenly (Vision!) the next step becomes lucidly clear.

The world calls the breakthrough "a gift." And it is, but the genius realizes that the gift came as a *result*, the reward for study, mental effort and thought. Hear the words of Alexander Graham Bell:

> What this power is I cannot say. All I know is that it exists. And it becomes available when a man is in that state of mind when he knows exactly what he wants and is fully determined not to quit until he finds it.

You don't get a million-dollar answer from a five-cent prayer. Neither do you get inspiration, insight or vision without sustained mental effort. You have got to want it and seek it. You've got to apply concentrated focus.

PARALLELS IN LIGHT

If you are still viewing focused attention as one of those "nice-but-not-necessary" qualities, consider what you could really gain by eliminating mental lapses.

As you recall, thought is a form of light (Chapter 4), and light exists in degrees. Not all light is the same, but includes a wide spectrum from gross forms (like incandescent and fluorescent) to very refined grades (like thought and knowledge). Intriguing parallels exist between the various degrees of light. Each has its own frequency, which dictates unique characteristics, yet the laws of one form of light apply just as directly to others. For example, concentration increases power, and diffusion dissipates power.

A laser is a device which amplifies the power of a narrow band of light frequencies. It produces a thin beam, so intense it can burn a hole through a diamond. Other forms of light, such as the light from florescent lamps and from the sun, spread in all directions. Laser light is focused, it travels in a single, concentrated direction. The power comes from concentration.

The parallels are striking. Thought, a high form of light, becomes more powerful when concentrated. Concentrated thinking produces greater results than diffused thinking. Pick your topics carefully. Then zero in.

CHAPTER 15

Commit to Commitment

A disciple once came to an Eastern master and said, "Master, I have two questions: What is the source of strength and power? And, what is the source of peace and serenity?"

"Your questions are not two, but one," replied the master, "and your answer is not two, but one."

The eager student pondered for a moment, and then replied, "I do not understand."

"Even so," affirmed the master, "you will understand, and will find the source when you, yourself, are no longer two, but one."

If you are not quite sure about the answer the master gave the disciple, the following may help. Have you noticed the duplicity between what people promise and what they fulfill?

A little duplicity exists in all of us. We function as though we are two people. One "person" makes a slate of commitments, many of them inattentively. Another "person" does what he or she feels like doing at the moment, keeping only a part of the promises. We're two, not one.

The master suggested greater wisdom. A vault full of qualities, from strength to serenity, comes from striving for oneness. He advised his disciple to curb the duplicity between promises and performance—to become one with himself, to be his word.

WHEN WORDS AND DEEDS ARE ONE

Integrity is not popular. As a society, we are known for seeking loopholes. When we do, we forfeit a unique combination of benefits. Keeping commitments, honoring our own word, doing what we say we'll do—enthroning integrity—leads to superlative states of mind. Strength and serenity, power and peace, come from *committing to commitment.*

Is your word your bond? Do you honor your own pledges? Are you moving toward oneness with your promises? Are you like Machiavelli or more like Pythias?

Machiavelli extolled expediency. To him, a person's word was merely a tactic; promises could be broken at any time if it furthered selfish purposes. Conditions would ultimately dictate actions. Whatever it took to accomplish the ends was justified. He believed that it mattered not what you did or said, as long as you got what you wanted.

Pythias, a fourth century Roman, lived above Machiavelli's plane. He honored all his commitments; his word was his law. Pythias' words and his deeds had become one. When he spoke a pledge, it was as good as done.

So consistent and dependable was his integrity all who knew Pythias could bet their lives on his word. Pythias' best friend, Damon, did just that. Pythias had run afoul of a tyrant, Dionysius, and was sentenced to die. Pythias had given his word to several people and wished to settle his affairs before he died.

Dionysius was persuaded to let Damon stand in place of Pythias. Damon promised to die in Pythias' stead, if Pythias failed to return. Dionysius thought Damon was a fool for placing so much trust in his friend's word. However, true to his commitment, Pythias returned in time to resume his own place at the execution. He had fulfilled his word to his creditors and all of his friends, including Damon, and was ready to die. Moved by Pythias' integrity, Dionysius released them both.

The legend of Damon and Pythias is frequently told as an example of great friendship, but it is really a story about integrity. Pythias lived his commitments. He was his word.

THE UNIVERSE REWARDS INTEGRITY

Integrity is golden. Literally and figuratively more precious than rubies, we attain it as we seek it. Developing integrity, the portal to personal empowerment, happens incrementally, a step at a time. Yet the moment you make a strong commitment to strive for it, you acquire power! What counts most is your commitment to improve on this principle.

Commit to commitment! Watch what you say; strive to do what you say; and then, watch what happens. You gain power. Power over yourself, power to influence and strengthen others, power to reach higher goals, and power to shape more directly the events around you.

The converse is equally true. The sloppier you are with your commitments, the weaker you will be personally, the less influence you will wield with others, and the less impact you will have on the world outside.

The universe rewards integrity! The principle is both direct and proportionate. The degree to which your desires and requests are granted corresponds, directly and proportionately, to your level of integrity. Even immediate small changes have immediate effect. The more commitments you keep, the more your own requests will be fulfilled. Simple equation.

Steven F. Hardison has many talents. He has been a record-setting salesman for such giants as Xerox and Procter & Gamble. Just recently he was president of Rodel Products Corporation. One of his best known traits is his dedication to living his word.

He says:

> I am committed to be my word for the simple reason that it
> is insanity not to. I believe you get back in life exactly what
> you put out there.

I agree with him; you reap in life what you sow. When you impute value to your word, your word returns the value manyfold.

The "boy who cried 'wolf'" lost power. He forfeited the strength he could have derived from others who would have acted on his behalf based solely on his word. Directly opposite, your words can become forceful vectors of creation, when you establish an impeccable state of integrity. When others can trust what you say, your words create rippling spheres of influence.

People weaken themselves when they blame circumstances; they become strong as they keep their word despite circumstances. People like Steve Hardison understand the principle, and they work at keeping their commitments no matter what. They strive for oneness between word and deed to such a degree that stunning "coincidences" happen for them on a frequent basis. They believe in direct and proportionate reward for integrity, sensing that most coincidences in life are not coincidental.

Steve has experienced rewards for his integrity several times. One example occurred while he was in Dallas, Texas, on business. Having made a commitment to be at a meeting in Phoenix that evening at 7:30 p.m., he had planned with his travel agent accordingly. A flight had been booked to leave Dallas-Fort Worth Airport (DFW) in the late afternoon with enough leeway to allow him to arrive on time for his meeting.

Complications arose. By the time Steve was dropped off at the airport, his flight was departing. The gate door was closed, the plane had pushed back. No way would he be on that plane.

Most people would have said, "Well I did my best. I tried to be on time for my meeting. Circumstances, events and other people precluded me from keeping my commitment." Steve did not excuse himself so easily. He has developed a tenacious desire to keep every promise. (Not that he is perfect. He's on the learning curve, too.)

Steve had missed his scheduled flight, yet his commitment still stood. He acted fast. He ran back to the counter and said, "I have to be in Phoenix at 7:30. I missed my flight. Is there any other flight departing DFW, so I can be in Phoenix on time?"

The agent scanned the schedules. There was only one other flight. Another airline, in a different terminal, was scheduled to depart in 10 minutes. "There is no way you can physically get to that terminal, check in, exchange your ticket and make that flight," said the agent.

"We'll see," said Steve, as he dashed down the corridor.

If you have been to DFW, you know it is large and sprawling. It was a miracle Steve even got to the gate in that short amount of time. But he did. Racing to the gate, he found a queue of angry, disgruntled people lined up at the counter. An agent was speaking into the microphone, explaining that the flight had been over-booked, and there were not enough seats for everyone who wanted passage.

Again, most people would have caved in at that point, saying, "Oh well, I did my best. What more can you expect?" Steve bypassed the line of people who were accepting the circumstances and complaining about customer service, and went directly to the attendant at the gate. The plane, mind you, is fully booked, fully loaded and ready to push back. Steve looked the man directly in the eye and calmly, but firmly, stated, "I do not have time to explain. I just must be in Phoenix at 7:30."

Here is the moment of decision. The universe is in gear. Circumstances are in motion. Events are moving to their appointed completion. One human being, Steve Hardison, needs to adjust things a bit, and has made the request. Will this request be granted or denied?

The principle of direct and proportionate reward for integrity now comes into play. Steve has recently logged a high batting average of fulfillment. That which goes around, comes around; and (CLICK) the universe rewards.

The attendant did not ask one question. He said to Steve, "Come with me." They walked down the jetway to the plane. The attendant grabbed the microphone and stated, "I have to buy a seat on this flight. There will be hotel accommodations provided and a free round-trip ticket to any destination in the continental United States, if someone will give up his or her seat." There was a pause. (The universe sometimes pauses in its movements for dramatic effect.) Then slowly a hand rose into the air. A woman accepted the attendant's offer.

Steve looked the attendant in the eye, thanked him, and handed him a ticket—but one for another airline. That could have been the last straw, could have thwarted the whole chain of events; but it didn't. The attendant knew how to handle the transfer, did not blink an eye but wished Steve a safe flight. He walked away holding Steve's ticket, escorting the woman who had given up her seat to the counter to fulfill the airline's promise to her. (Good airlines know and observe the principle of integrity, too.)

In this simple experience, one large issue needs highlight. In the overall course of human events, whether Steve made that plane and attended the meeting in Phoenix, seems utterly inconsequential. That event, fulfilled or unfulfilled, would not appear to monumentally alter the course of history. Thousands of meetings occur every day where someone who committed to be there doesn't show up. The universe appears to proceed unimpressed and undeterred. But that is where we miss the point. The universe actually *has* been affected.

When keeping commitments becomes a priority in people's lives, just consequences ensue. A beneficial pattern of events, which they have caused, also establishes patterns of effects which return to them in kind. (What goes around, comes around.)

Each time they give their word, even in very simple things, like making an appointment or returning a call, they keep it. The universe is affected, however so slightly, by their mind and their actions, and duly takes note. Small victories add up. Potential energy accrues. The energy waits in abeyance, ready to be accessed later on.

If Steve's appointment in Phoenix was not the pivotal event in saving the entire free world, why did all these occurrences fall into place for Steve Hardison? Was it all just happenstance? A matter of coincidence? Luck? I submit not. Something higher was at stake, and higher powers were at work.

Through this process of keeping commitments, Steve has not only gained strength, he has aligned himself with the law of direct and proportionate reward. It stood primed, ready to move in his favor. Suddenly, when the chips were down, he had the right to ask for, and to receive, a favorable response to his request. The universe moved and granted the request.

Goethe recognized the relationship between firm commitment and "coincidences":

> [The] moment one **definitely commits oneself**, then Providence moves too. All sorts of things occur to help one that would never otherwise have occurred. A whole stream of events issues from the decision, raising in one's favor all manner of unforeseen incidents and meetings and material assistance, which no man could have dreamed would come his way.

Quite likely, you have run across this oft-quoted statement. Perhaps you have thought of it in terms of a single event, such as the setting of a goal. That is the way I first saw this statement. I later saw something more. If you look at commitment as a policy, an engrafted way of living, rather than an event, it takes on far greater power. As your integrity in all things increases, favorable "streams of events," flowing in your favor, will increase. And the flow is direct and proportionate.

KEEP EVERY PROMISE, LARGE AND SMALL

Make no mistake about it. Something very definite and very real takes place every time you keep a promise. It strengthens you. It adds power. You expand your capacity to accomplish bigger and better things.

Each promise kept adds and each failure subtracts—a simple and just equation. The greater and more difficult the commitment, the greater the degree of empowerment when fulfilled. However, no promise is so small or insignificant that keeping it won't add strength. The law of sequential growth applies here, too. Keeping "small" promises makes the greater possible.

In the final analysis, the determinant in life's battles is not complex: Strong people win; weak people lose. And, in practical terms, we can all move from weakness to strength by learning to keep covenants and promises.

THE CRUCIAL STEP OF AWARENESS

Most of us do not even recognize how many commitments and promises we make during the course of a day. Functioning as though they have no value, promises spew forth freely and without much care or thought. We overlook a good many of the commitments we make. We don't see them, but the universe does.

Many times we give our word and know, right at the time, that we have no real intention of keeping it. Encountering an old friend, for example, we say, "We really need to get together some time and go out to dinner."

"Yeh," replies the friend, "Why don't you give me a call sometime, and we'll set that up."

"Sure," we *promise*, **"I'll do that."** And of course we never do. We said we would call (gong: commitment spoken, word given) but we don't call; you never really intended to in the first place.

Getting together would be nice, but somehow it seems like more effort than it's worth. Besides, we are pretty sure that enough stuff (circumstances, events, and other requests) will clog both our memories. We'll both just forget about it, and things will drop. But one of the things that drops is integrity.

As illustrated in Section II, all those things that get in the way are factors or effects, and human beings are above all that. Factors do not control us, although most of us constantly rationalize that they do. The only thing really keeping us from fulfilling our commitments is us. So if we did not keep our word, it is simply because we did not do so. The oneness between what we say and what we do only comes down to how strongly we feel about it.

Whenever you say and then do, you amplify your integrity. Your confidence waxes stronger, leading to stronger states of mind. The kinetic and potential energy of the universe responds to such power, and you become a force therein. You can move things in your favor.

You can see why this prerequisite works as a potent precursor to the higher states of mind. To gain strength, think about what you say; say only what you really mean; then be your word.

EMPHASIZE COMMITMENT MANAGEMENT

Wherever you have been, wherever you now are on the integrity curve, commitment overcomes the past. Committing to commitment sets you in the forward direction and propels you forward. And **organization accelerates your pace!**

Organization pays. It immediately puts you in control and furnishes ways of documenting progress. No other step guarantees more consistent improvement or greater satisfaction.

Once again, an organizer provides simple, easy ways of doing it all. When you get your organizer, you're on your way. It helps heighten your awareness to the commitments you make, track them and be more rigorous with fulfillment. You get a little better—a little closer to being one with yourself—each passing day.

One facet of my portable office has been a huge practical aid in my quest to master the principle of commitment. As mentioned, my system has a pre-dated day page for every day of the year. Part of that page is designed to document and manage commitments. Entitled the TASK MASTER, it really functions as a COMMITMENT MANAGER. Whenever I speak a promise—to transmit a proposal or call a client—I flip forward to the day I promised to complete that commitment, and I formally jot it down on the Task Master.

This practice assists me in several ways. First, it elevates my awareness of when I am creating a commitment. I have, as a consequence, become more careful and thoughtful about what I agree to. I am not as flippant about agreements and promises. Before I give my word, I honestly consider my schedule, my previous commitments and my goals (all of which are also closely at hand in my organizer). I do not make the commitment unless I truthfully and realistically feel I can fulfill my word. That alone has been a major stride forward.

In addition, the Task Master helps me track the commitments to completion. This reminder system brings the tasks and commitments back to me, automatically. (The pre-dated day page system secures that.)

I can build any number of necessary notices into the system for managing even longer-range projects. The multiple components of each project, with their individual deadlines, can also be plotted onto the precise day.

Furthermore, I have a way of prioritizing each daily list. I can ensure that first things come first. Additionally, the system provides a superb way to delegate with a fool-proof follow-up system to guarantee completion.

I recommend you use a daily self-management system which will provide you with similar benefits. (If you are not currently using such a comprehensive system, I recommend you promptly repent and call 1-800-622-6463 and request information on the TimeMax Organizer.)

ENTHRONE COMMITMENT

Make up your mind to do what it takes to develop masterful integrity to your own word. Make "keeping your word" a dominant thought. Mind will drive body to total integrity. (Whatever you do, you do first in your mind.) Think about what you say. Say only what you really mean. Then be your word. Cease being double-minded, saying one thing and doing something else. Become one.

Bring yourself into a high level of integrity by really committing to commitment. Align yourself with the remarkable law of direct and proportionate reward: THE UNIVERSE REWARDS INTEGRITY!

CHAPTER 16

The Michelangelo Principle

As you steadily improve your mind management—vanquishing clutter, augmenting attention span, enhancing concentration, and being more rigorous with commitments—your payoffs grow. Your increased discipline summons power. As you hone your mind management, you become more proficient at visioneering, and visioneering opens the gate to higher realms.

The greatest prerogative of the human mind is the ability to envision mental images and translate them into physical reality. We can transform vision into verity—fantasy into fact. We possess the incredible capability of constructing images in the present (now) which can travel ahead in time to govern and shape the future (then). Vision can transcend time, surmount obstacles, compress distances and move into the future, reproducing an exact replica of itself in physical form.

ON FAITH

To exercise this extraordinary capability of the mind, to translate images into their physical replica, is what I call "visioneering." Visioneering, the engineering of dreams into reality through sensory-rich mental imaging, renews an ancient concept of unspeakable value. The ability to foresee, and believe in, the reality of (as yet) unseen things, has been called in some contexts, "faith." Faith, a perfectly good word, would be my preference actually, were it not for the fact that for some it comes with so much extra cargo.

The word, faith, has lost its original potency, having become diluted by imprecise usages. Many people today think of faith in a religious context only, and equate it with a blind acceptance of some dogma, doctrine or theology. Furthermore, in that same context, the term has come to imply passive mental consent *only*. Mere agreement. Acceptance.

The word, faith, originally implied and conveyed so much more than blind acceptance. It implied power. And that's the point: Mental assent, acknowledgement or endorsement of some idea may be a start, but it lacks strength. Ironically, the modern dilution of the definition actually contradicts the very intent of the original word.

Faith, in its authentic definition, was descriptive of a state of mental power—a state of sufficient force to generate firm action and internal energy—a state sufficient to exert power over external elements. Faith, in that form, could move mountains.

Hence, I offer you a word which can be defined clean and fresh in your mind. Visioneering, a noun, has the flavor of a verb. It connotes **action coupled with defined purpose,** uniting the elements of **vision** (creative foresight) with **engineering** (the systemic application of laws and principles).

Combining the elements of vision and disciplined action, the word, visioneering, comes as close as I can devise to transmitting the essence of an incredibly important state of mind—a state of being and a state of power. My final objective in this book is to teach you what visioneering is, what it can do for you, and how to develop your ability to use it.

THE MICHELANGELO PRINCIPLE

Visioneering begins with vision, the ability of the mind's eye to *literally see* that which is not yet physically present. In my seminars I refer to this trait as The Michelangelo Principle:

MASTERS SEE THEIR CREATIONS BEFORE THEY ARE CREATED!

Among its many charms, Florence, Italy, is a renown center for the arts. I lived there for almost a year. Not then, and still not today, am I a great student of the arts. Back then, all I could tell you about "Art" was that it was short for Arthur.

I'd made up my mind, however, to visit these celebrated collections. The first I visited was the "Academia Delle Arte," housing one of the greatest collections in Europe.

We speak, in our everyday vernacular, of "breathtaking experiences." If you pick up a travel brochure or a real estate description and don't find the word "breathtaking" thrown into at least one paragraph, someone has missed some keys on the keyboard. If, however, you take that expression literally, I can tell you I have had only one or two truly breathtaking experiences in my life.

One I vividly remember happened at the Academia Delle Arte. The first large room of this museum was a deceptive prelude. Several famous paintings by the masters hung on the walls. A few sculptures posed in the middle of the floor. I meandered around, endeavoring to appreciate each one of these works as best I could.

Eventually, I strolled into a second or third room, a large one with a high, vaulted ceiling. My eyes immediately went to the walls, where I expected to see more paintings. But the walls were bare. No paintings at all.

Suddenly I realized there was only one work of art in the entire room. Right in the center of this huge chamber loomed the most imposing figure I have ever seen. Italians call it "Il

Gigante" (The Giant). Most of the rest of the world knows this towering work of the master, Michelangelo, as the "David."

Awestruck, I actually found myself skipping a breath. The elegance of this masterpiece bombarded my senses. No photograph or slide can do it justice. If you have not seen the "David" in person, you have missed a rare, unrepeatable experience. You have to stand there yourself to appreciate the imposing size and to feel how real and alive the figure is. You would swear it breathes.

On closer inspection, the awe increases. The perfect detail overwhelms. You not only see the definition of muscles in the legs, you see veins and tendons in the hands, wrists and feet. All the while, you remind yourself that some human being chipped, chiseled, carved this figure out of dense, unrelenting marble.

Take a chisel some time; lay it to marble. Then strike it with a hammer, and you will learn how unforgiving this substance is. How anyone could take a piece of rock and turn it into something so sublime, is almost beyond comprehension.

Captivated by the "David," I looked into the history of its creation. The story behind the statue makes it even more impressive.

In 1501, the city-state of Florence commissioned Michelangelo to create a giant statue. They intended, for political reasons, to position it in a prominent city square. Michelangelo accepted the commission. One patron suggested he consider a particular block of marble. A huge block of white marble, "over nine arm lengths long," had languished around Florence for quite some time. Quarried in Carrara a hundred years previously, the block had attracted the attention of lesser artists from time to time.

By the time Michelangelo came to inspect the immense chunk of marble, it had been badly damaged and distorted. Michelangelo's biographer, Vasari, writes the following description:

> The marble was eighteen feet high, but unfortunately an
> artist called Simone da Fiesole had started to carve a giant
> figure and had bungled the work so badly that he had
> hacked a hole between the legs and left the block com-
> pletely botched and misshapen.

Many people considered the block unfit for a masterpiece. Some spoke of breaking it down or of adding pieces, so
some artful use could come of it. Others, pronouncing it ruined,
suggested abandoning the block altogether. Their minds could
not see, lying silently within this malformed, disfigured material,
the superb potential physique of the "David." Unable to see it,
they could not create it.

Michelangelo was a master where the others were not.
His ability to see what others could not set him apart. Others
were caught in the "is" of the moment. Michelangelo could see
beyond "what is" to envision "what could be."

Historians say he studied the block carefully—measuring
and assessing. But much more went on there in those moments
of decision than abstract mathematical calculations.
Michelangelo had to see, project, visualize.

If you really think about it, you can picture it too: The
master sculptor, slowly walking along the length of the marble,
musing, thinking. Pausing at one end, he studies and ponders.
Moving pensively along the other side, he observes the flaws and
the position of the hole in the marble. At the other end he
freezes, deliberating, contemplating, deeply immersed in
thought. His gaze penetrates into the center of the stone itself.

Then, after what seems like an eternity, he looks up, and
he knows! This is the block! The flaws do not cut through the
figure in the stone! **The master can see the creation before it's
created.**

The "David" lives so vividly in his mind, he can see the
dimensions, the pose, the posture. He can project that image into

the stony reality of the marble before him. It's there! He can see it; nothing has to be added. The flaws are irrelevant.

The mental creation was complete and would govern the physical creation. Before the hammer and chisels went to work, "Il Gigante" had been created. The "David" lived. It lived in Michelangelo's mind. His whole philosophy about sculpting was that the figures already existed in the stone. His role was to see them, and then remove the clutter—the excess, the covering—and liberate the captives within.

The story of the "David" is enlightening and dramatic. A master sculptor, looking beyond the surface, looking beyond the cracks and blemishes, sees what others cannot. Overlooking what is, he creates, out of chaos, a masterpiece.

The example is dramatic but not exceptional. The principle holds true in myriad settings and contexts. Not just a quaint story from art history, Michelangelo's creation of "David" epitomizes one of the important elements of creation—Visioneering. Furthermore, never has there been, nor ever will there be, a great business, an outstanding achievement, a lofty goal, an ingenious invention, a monumental breakthrough or a noble life which has not been brought into being through this process I call visioneering.

The more I study high achievers and successful people in all walks of life, the clearer it becomes. They visualize in graphic detail the outcomes they intend to produce. They create their masterpieces visually, then physically.

VISUALIZATION

Children are natural dreamers. Look back at your own childhood. When you came into this world, you possessed a vivid imagination. You had a prolific, well-developed capacity for creativity. You could play Vikings, cops and robbers, carry on imaginary conversations with animals and fictitious people in great detail.

Somewhere along the line, this society douses that talent. We are encouraged to become analytical and logical. While those traits are important and merit cultivation, we tend to downplay and neglect our imaginary, visionary capacity. Visualization is not just child's play! It is the great triggering mechanism of the human creative genius.

Nikolai Tesla, considered by many to be one of the keenest, creative minds of the 20th century, was a notable visioneer. Tesla could not only construct inventions in his mind's eye, he could actually "operate" them mentally. He was able to see if they would work, and troubleshoot most of the "bugs" in his inventions, before he actually put them together physically. A classic example of The Michelangelo Principle in action, Tesla confirms how literally mental creation precedes and precipitates physical creation.

Other experiences of Nikolai Tesla verify two of our premises: (1) discipline and effort prepare the way for higher powers, and (2) these powers can be cultivated.

Tesla's mother worked with her son to develop his mental skills at an early age. She played visualization games with him almost daily. She would have him close his eyes while she read parts of stories to him. Little Nikolai would envision the scenes in vivid detail, and then his mother would have him go on and describe the rest of the story and create how the plot would unfold. Mother Tesla insisted that he be thorough and graphic in his narratives.

As this exercise continued, Nikolai's mother began to notice something extraordinary. After a while, Nikolai's intuitive powers began to develop and became increasingly evident.

At first Nikolai's versions of the stories he visualized were unique and had no likeness to the parts of the story which his mother had not yet read. But as time went on, Nikolai's versions began to coincide with the unread portions in the books. Dismissing this at first as mere coincidence, the occurrences became the rule rather than the exception. Eventually his accuracy in predicting the rest of the plot became uncanny.

Ms. Tesla became convinced that her son was a genius and started treating him as such. She called him "her little genius" (and guess what began to be one of his dominant thoughts?).

She did not let his "gifts" lie dormant. Ms. Tesla began to work to directly cultivate his intuitive powers. With a blindfold in place, she would have him discern colors without using his physical eyes. She would hold pieces of colored cloth or paper behind his head and ask him to sense what the color was. Within months, Nikolai became phenomenally accurate.

Even in his adult years, Nikolai retained his blindfolded color perception ability. Performing this feat at gatherings, he would amaze friends and acquaintances.

STEPHEN HAWKING

Some people would say that the greatest mind of the second half of the 20th century is Stephen W. Hawking of Great Britain. A marvelous theoretical physicist, he has taken over where Albert Einstein left off and has revolutionized our concepts of the universe.

Afflicted with a terribly aggressive disease, Hawking's body has virtually become a prison. He cannot at this point sign his name or speak. Hawking communicates through a voice synthesizer which he controls with one thumb and forefinger. In a strange way, this disease has been a benefit, both to him and to the rest of mankind. His disability has forced him to concentrate. Note what his mother, Isobel Hawking, observed:

> He says himself that he wouldn't have got where he is if he hadn't been ill...he has concentrated on this in a way I don't think he would have otherwise, because he always took a great interest in a lot of things in life and I don't know that

he'd ever have applied himself in the same way if he'd been able to get around. So, in a way...no, I can't say anyone's lucky to have an illness like that, but it's less bad luck for him than it would be for some people, because he can live so much in his head.

Interestingly, Stephen Hawking's disease has been advantageous in one other way. It has virtually required him to develop and cultivate The Michelangelo Principle. Note what Kip Thorne, one of Stephen's colleagues, says:

As Stephen gradually lost the use of his hands, he had to start developing geometrical arguments that he could do pictorially in his head. He developed a very powerful set of tools that nobody else really had.

We can all learn from Hawking. He, again, demonstrates that mental skills are developable. To some degree, at least, we can emulate him. Obviously, I am not advocating that we formulate physical disabilities, but I recommend we learn to visualize more effectively.

The more Hawking was forced to visualize, the more prolific became his creative output. An unmistakable correlation exists there. Visualization was the key attribute which led to the remarkable breakthroughs Hawking has produced. And, that which applies to him applies to you and me.

Cultivate The Michelangelo Principle in your own life. Hear it, O ye ends of the earth! *Vision* is the catalyst which links and ignites all other faculties of the human being. Vision is the component which unites, directs and fuels the effective performance of body, sensations and passions.

You will soon see why.

CHAPTER 17

The Conscious and Subconscious

We all sense that much more goes on inside our minds than just conscious thoughts. Over the years, you have undoubtedly noticed multiple levels of mental activity.

The body, for example, with all its complex functions, perks right along without much conscious attention. Yet conscious thoughts can (and do) have instantaneous impact on behavior. While you are reading this book, some subconscious level operates your heart and lungs, yet, with conscious will, you can shift yourself into gear and move to the refrigerator to gulp some yogurt. Some non-conscious level of mind runs the body, and yet, at will, you can consciously intervene.

At other times we find ourselves dwelling on a certain subject, and suddenly another idea bursts into our conscious awareness, completely out of the blue. That flash of insight seems to come from an entirely different plane than our conscious thoughts. (And it does.)

You may have seen that, even while dreaming, there are levels of thinking. Sometimes we seem to be dreaming randomly, aimlessly. At other times, we are dreaming on one specific topic and, even while sleeping, are able, from a higher level, to direct our dreams to other themes.

Anyone who has had experience with hypnosis has discovered two distinct planes or levels. Our normal, behavior-governing level (call it the conscious mind) is circumvented and another very obedient and impressionable level (call it the subconscious mind) is accessed. This impressionable level of mind can carry out instructions in flawless detail without help from our conscious mind.

In summary, our own experience, along with ample clinical evidence, points to multiple levels of mental activity. For our present purposes, we will focus on two levels and call them:

(1) The Conscious Level

(2) The Subconscious Level

Henceforth, throughout this book, I will refer to these levels as though they were separate minds. This is for instructive purposes only. Obviously, in reality, they are not separate minds; they are aspects of the overall whole, the indivisible human psyche. This partitioning, though artificial, will further our understanding and simplify our discussion.

OF CAPTAINS

We begin with a simple analogy. Picture a fleet of cargo ships. Each ship has a captain, standing on the bridge, evaluating incoming data. The captains view the horizon; they have guidance instruments and compasses in front of them; and they have training and past experience to draw upon. Based on this "data base," these captains continually make value judgments and decisions which affect the entire vessel. They determine destinations, courses, speeds and the timing of the voyage.

Somewhat analogously, your conscious mind functions as the "captain of your mental ship." It considers, sorts and analyzes vast amounts of data. Comparable to a ship's instruments, your conscious mind deals with a very active

guidance system—a spiritual-moral values system or con-
science. Concepts of right and wrong, good and bad, success and
failure are largely the domain of your conscious mind; and it
tussles with these issues constantly.

Based on the incoming data and the value system, your
conscious mind selects targets and destinations, bearings and
routes, speeds and timing of your goals and activities. In short,
decisions and judgments regarding your behavior are largely the
province of the conscious mind.

OF CREWS

On ships, once captains make a decision, other members
of the staff stir into action. While the captains retain ultimate
responsibility, they do not actually implement the orders. They
do not reach for oars and attempt to propel the ship. Instead, they
radio down to the unseen world below deck where crews stand
poised and ready to obey the captains' orders. The crews make
no value judgments. If the crews were to exercise opinions and
options of their own, shipwreck would result. Crews have the
systems operating and ready, but they put nothing into gear
without orders from above. They are trained to implement precisely and exactly what comes from the bridge. *

The crews are analogous to your subconscious mind.
The subconscious functions as crew to the conscious mind and
works faithfully to implement orders. It does so obediently,
dutifully and without question.

One more element of the ship analogy has merit. Where
does the real dynamic propulsion of the ship originate? Not from
the captain. Captains initiate, but the power to drive the vessel
comes from engines down below deck. Similarly, the real power
in the human being—your creative sources, your energy sources,
the drives of your body—are handled by subconscious sectors,
"down below deck."

---

*Recent computerized control systems have strengthened the analogy. When the officer on the
bridge orders, human crews no longer implement them. Human error and judgment (other than
the captains') is completely circumvented. Electronic control systems ensure immediate and
accurate response to the orders.

Thus successful human "navigation" is a team effort. Each component of the team has a rightful, individual function, but the members work interdependently. And, they are nothing short of awesome when they work synergistically.

CLARIFYING THE CONTRASTS

The simple ship analogy gets us launched, but further detail regarding these two sectors of the mind sheds more light on the mechanisms of Visioneering. Let me, therefore, briefly list and explain some of the respective prerogatives of the conscious and subconscious minds.

THE CONSCIOUS MIND: "Captain of the mental ship."

(1) Personal.

Your conscious mind constitutes the part of the mind you are most familiar with. You generally associate it with your very personality. You think of it as the "me" inside—your individual identity. And it certainly is. However, there is more of "you" than the conscious sector, as you will soon see.

(2) Locus of rational or deliberate thought.

The conscious mind is the site of most of your waking monologue. The so-called "rational" or cognitive conversations going on inside your head are conscious thoughts. As you read this page, you formulate sounds of words in your conscious mind. As you pause to consider ideas, reasoning and assessing, you carry on internal discourses in that same conscious sector.

(3) **Subject to voluntary control.**

You have total control over the moment-by-moment workings of your conscious mind. To me, the most amazing capability of the human mind (and I continue to marvel at this property) is the ability to think about what we're thinking, right in the process of thinking it; and change any time we wish.

We are constantly self-diagnosing. We continually assess our thoughts, determining whether to continue thinking along those lines or switch to something else. Our control over conscious thinking is complete and absolute.

(4) **Possesses a prominent value system.**

Your conscious mind possesses a prominent spiritual-moral value system. It wrestles constantly with the issues of "good and bad," "right and wrong," "workable and unworkable."

(5) **Makes value judgments and evaluations.**

Based on the foregoing point, it becomes obvious that the conscious mind continually makes value judgments and evaluations. The conscious mind assesses its own thoughts according to this value system, and also, judges the "outside world" by the same criteria.

(6) **Makes decisions and selects destinations.**

Assessing all the incoming data, making decisions and judgments, the conscious mind determines destinations. Whatever you say, whatever you do, you select first in your conscious sector. (Behavior, you recall, is mind driving body in fulfillment of consciously selected dominant thoughts.)

Obviously much more could be written about the captain and grand decision-maker, the conscious mind. Yet, even if we catalogued all its faculties and capabilities, we would have but a small portion of the story if we neglected other levels of mental activity. Knowledge of the conscious mind is but the preamble.

THE SUBCONSCIOUS MIND: "Crew of the mental ship."

(1) Impersonal.

As curious as this may seem at first, your subconscious mind functions, in most respects, as a dispassionate, disinterested third party. It participates as requested and directed, but does not take things "personally." (More on that shortly.)

(2) Locus of highly creative, innovative thought.

The creative capacity and innovative ability of the subconscious is stunning. The conscious mind hardly holds a candle to the brilliance of the subconscious when it comes to problem-solving and invention. The subconscious is the site of your creative genius.

(3) Does not override conscious thought.

Although in many respects more potent and capable, the subconscious functions in a subordinate role to the conscious mind. Ordinarily, the subconscious does not override, interrupt or cover "conversations" going on in the conscious mind. It tends, rather, to interject information between thoughts, and functions best when the conscious mind is not harried, occupied or busy. (Relating this to the chapter on clutter, you can see the wisdom of the recommendations therein.)

(4) Subject to secondary or indirect control.

Some people have suggested that the subconscious is a wild horse that runs totally unbridled, all by itself. Nothing could be further from the truth. You can control your subconscious, but that control is not as perfect, complete and direct as that which you have in the conscious sector.

(5) **Does not possess a prominent moral value system.**

In marked contrast to the conscious mind, the subconscious does not grapple with concepts of "right and wrong," "feasible and unfeasible," the way the conscious mind does. This does not mean the subconscious is valueless, immoral or amoral. It simply does not concern itself with ethical issues.

(6) **Makes no value judgments.**

Since the subconscious does not concern itself with a value system, it does not make value judgments. That function is left entirely up to the conscious. The subconscious concerns itself with results, not morality.

(7) **Does not initiate pursuits.**

Reject the postulate that conscious behavior derives from dark, repressed (mostly sexually-oriented) memories in the subconscious. (Sorry, Sigmund, wrong alley.) The conscious mind exerts sovereign control and holds full sway. It operates as the instigator of behavior; the subconscious functions as the implementor. And that stands as a crucial distinction. The subconscious does not initiate pursuits; rather it responds to pursuits. Very obedient and totally subservient to the dominant thoughts selected by the conscious mind, it works in a subordinate capacity.

With this working knowledge of the parameters and prerogatives of the conscious and the subconscious, we are prepared to study the remarkable interdependent relationship between these two creative counterparts.

CHAPTER 18

Creative Counterparts

Some things we do so automatically, so naturally, we rarely notice them. Nevertheless, taking the time to analyze pays off. Understanding leads to control, and control leads to precise applications with more dependable results.

Breathing, for example, is one of the most automatic things we do, and yet, greater understanding leads to useful techniques, yielding better outcomes. Women preparing for childbirth learn to mitigate pain through focused breathing techniques. Refined methods of breathing enhance relaxation and meditation abilities in yoga. Musicians, vocalists and athletes, all learn to improve performance by increasing their skills in the simple, natural act of breathing. Applied knowledge improves performance.

Like the simple matter of breathing, the mechanisms of behavior work quite automatically. They function so rapidly and smoothly, we hardly recognize the process. These intricate mechanisms hub around a marvelously effective relationship between our conscious and subconscious minds.

Understanding how these two creative counterparts interface—how they check and balance one another, how they mutually support and enhance one another, how they brilliantly combine to effectuate creativity and behavior—opens the door to remarkable advances. Both sectors work *interdependently and synergistically* and play crucial roles in creating behavior.

This remarkable relationship rests on four premises:

- 1 -

CONSCIOUS MIND ACTIVATES SUBCONSCIOUS MIND WITH DOMINANT THOUGHT

The conscious mind (captain) commands, and the sub-conscious mind (crew) takes orders. An orderly hierarchy presides in your internal world. The conscious acts as architect; the subconscious serves as contractor.

Ultimate responsibility lies with the conscious mind. Your subconscious mind does not decide behavior. Neither is it a loose cannon that can go off all by itself. The subconscious *does* work on subjects while the conscious mind is elsewhere occupied. But the topics which the subconscious works on have been previously designated and stipulated *by prior activity* in the conscious mind.

Were it not so, none of us could be held accountable for our actions, (which is precisely why many propound this erroneous doctrine) and the issues of self-control, self-discipline and personal responsibility would be shams.

The subconscious mind is impersonal and impres-sionable, completely open to suggestion. In terms of subject matter, the subconscious mind is totally passive, and depends upon the conscious mind for direction. Every consciously repeated idea or image exerts an effect, supplying direction to the subconscious. Like a garden, fertile and freshly-tilled, your sub-conscious accepts whatever seeds you plant. Any seed will grow and thrive therein. If you plant wheat, you'll get wheat. And if you plant weeds, you'll get weeds.

Maxwell Maltz, M.D., taught this concept in his well-respected book, *Psycho-cybernetics*, published in 1960. Dr. Maltz wrote:

> The Creative Mechanism [*read "subconscious mind"*] within you is impersonal. It will work automatically and impersonally to achieve goals of success and happiness, or unhappiness and failure, depending upon the goals which you yourself set for it. Present it with "success goals" [*positive dominant thoughts*] and it functions as a "Success Mechanism." Present it with negative goals, [*negative dominant thoughts*] and it operates just as impersonally, and just as faithfully as a "Failure Mechanism."

"Garbage in, garbage out," a phrase well-known to computer programmers, also works as a sure principle of the mind; and so does, "Goodness in, goodness out."

The subconscious mind makes no value judgments. It will not reject inferior thoughts, and substitute superior ones; it does not even recognize the difference. Your conscious mind can do that, but the subconscious cannot.

By dwelling on a thought, any thought, in your conscious mind, you dispatch orders to the subconscious to align with that very thought. Whatever you imprint, the subconscious dutifully accepts. For better or for worse.

From that point on, automatic mechanisms of implementation move into action to bring that idea into reality. WHATEVER THE CONSCIOUS MIND DWELLS ON, THE SUBCONSCIOUS MIND ACTS ON.

EXERTING CONTROL ON THE SUBCONSCIOUS

This critical realization casts light on how you can exert intelligent control over your subconscious behavior. Since the subconscious cannot induce, only deduce, it stands in the subservient role. It must receive orders and take directions from the conscious mind. Those orders are given in the form of dominant thoughts. Thus, it follows: To take direct control of your dominant thoughts is to exert indirect control of your subconscious agenda!

Dominant thought management not only governs your deliberate, rational, conscious thinking but the creative, innovative thinking of your subconscious as well. And, it even goes well beyond that, as you will soon see.

- 2 -

Once the subconscious mind is stimulated or activated with a dominant thought, what is it stimulated to do? First, and perhaps foremost, it *generates plans.*

SUBCONSCIOUS MIND DEVELOPS PLANS TO REALIZE DOMINANT THOUGHT

The subconscious acts as the great innovator. Present it with a specific objective and, immediately, it goes to work designing solutions and pathways forward. It becomes a fountainhead of plans and designs targeted at translating the idea or image into its physical or behavioral equivalent. The subconscious creates the bridge of ideas, spanning the chasm from present state to desired destination.

Undoubtedly, you can relate to the familiar experience of having, out of the blue, an ingenious idea suddenly pop onto center stage. Into your cognizant awareness comes the perfect answer to a problem you want to solve or the pathway to a goal you want to achieve. Like a bolt of lightening (zzzappp), illumination arrives! These sudden bursts of insight are bulletins from the creative sector of your mind. The subconscious mind has delivered a plan developed in response to a prior dominant thought.

Frequently, such insights burst unexpectedly. Some of them occur at downright inconvenient moments, like when you are standing in the shower or driving your car. Do you know why they happen then? Those are two times when you cannot write them in your organizer. (Just funning.)

The explanation for these sudden, seemingly serendipitous, flashes of brilliance goes back to the conscious-subconscious relationship. As stated before, the subconscious does not, ordinarily, override deliberate, purposeful conscious thought. However, when the conscious mind is relaxed and unoccupied, the subconscious can take the initiative and can flash plans and insights onto center stage.

Another common occurrence casts light on the subconscious mind's planning activities. You may have gone to sleep, thinking about a specific goal or a puzzle you want to solve. In the middle of the night, you awaken with the answer flowing in your mind. Or, you have the idea burst, spontaneously, into mind upon rising the next morning. Some very respectable ideas have undoubtedly come to you in this fashion.

Most of us grossly underestimate our own creative ability. We timidly decline the designation "genius," attributing such intellect to others. Yet, geniuses obtain their sparkling insights the same way you and I do—using the same mechanism described here. Focusing their conscious thought on a particular topic, they set the subconscious mind into action. Pondering from time to time, they reinforce the search for that particular answer or breakthrough. Suddenly, bolting onto center stage, comes an answer. Having searched, probed, parsed, winnowed and sifted a vast array of potentials and possibilities, the creative sector offers a plan for consideration.

German chemist, Friedrich Kekule, on an autumn evening in 1865, sat dozing in front of a warm fire. For weeks he had been pondering a specific dilemma, the configuration of the molecule, benzene. Suddenly, into his relaxed mind, came a vision of gyrating chains of atoms.

One of the chains twisted, he reported, in a serpentine manner:

> One of the snakes had seized hold of its own tail, and the form whirled mockingly before my eyes. As if roused by a flash of lightening, I awoke.

Kekule had received his solution. His now well-known discovery, the benzene ring, forms the basis of modern organic chemistry.

Kekule's experience illustrates the innovative interplay between the conscious mind and the subconscious mind; and it is nothing short of miraculous. Having given his creative center specific orders, his subconscious had gone to work. After a period of gestation in which ideas were sorted and organized, the subconscious presented a solution.

This phenomenon works consistently throughout the human race. Thomas Edison, Marie Curie, and Albert Einstein received their ingenious ideas via the same method you receive yours. The principle is no respecter of persons.

Now that you are more aware of it, you will see the evidence all about you. The other day I was reading *The Money Game*, a book by Adam Smith. Referring to the key characteristic of successful money managers, he described the subconscious flashing process perfectly:

> Professional money managers often seem to make up their minds in a split second, but what pushes them over the line of decision is usually an incremental bit of information which, added to all the slumbering pieces of information filed in their minds, suddenly makes the picture whole.

A productive designer of electronic circuits, a man who had achieved many notable breakthroughs for his firm, described his breakthrough experiences like this:

> I focus intently on the problem at hand for a couple of hours. Then I walk away, clear my head and go on to

something else. When I come back, 15 to 20 minutes later, I see things there that I could have sworn weren't there before. My subconscious has been taking the variables, shuffling them and putting them back together.

Our subconscious genius works constantly. It operates so automatically, we take it for granted. But stop for a minute. Think of what a marvelous prerogative you possess. You can focus your attention on any subject you wish—select any topic, any subject—and by pondering and meditating upon it, you can call forth light and insight (genius) on that precise issue.

CHAPTER 19

Checks and Balances

What young child has not marvelled at the story of Aladdin and his magical lamp? We have all probably envied Aladdin and wanted to be able to call forth a genie to bestow upon us our hearts' desires. Yet, in effect, each one of us has that very privilege. The genie is real and is none other that the synergistic genius of your conscious and subconscious minds.

Here is the creative sequence thus far:

(1) Conscious Mind Activates Subconscious Mind With Dominant Thought.

(2) Subconscious Mind Develops Plans To Realize Dominant Thought.

Given a specific topic, the subconscious mind sends options back to the conscious mind. Why does the subconscious mind bother to do this? Why does it flash these ideas back to the conscious mind at all? If, as some contend, the subconscious is the ultimate determinant in human behavior, why does this well-known phenomenon—the referral of ideas back to the conscious mind—take place?

The answer is simple. The subconscious mind is not in charge. It functions as a dynamic creative designer, but ranks

subordinate to the conscious mind when it comes to implementation. A great system of checks and balances presides over this
interplay. The subconscious can go wild with zany possibilities,
but the conscious mind must approve the plan.

- 3 -

THE CONSCIOUS MIND EVALUATES THE PLANS

The innovations of the subconscious are flashed back to
the conscious for evaluation. Why? The conscious mind possesses a prominent value system, and the subconscious does not.
An idea must be validated by the conscious mind, *and be
approved*, before it can be converted to behavior.

The mechanisms of our behavior contain a system of
checks and balances. Dominant thoughts flow to the subconscious so naturally, and the subconscious works on them so automatically, the planning process is always going on. It all
proceeds so fluidly that overrides must exist.

The subconscious *never fails* to produce a plan. Every
dominant thought elicits a plan from the subconscious mind.
Even negative or evil thoughts make the circuit, resulting in
inappropriate plans coming back from the subconscious.

Most of us must admit that our subconscious has, from
time to time, presented some fairly colorful plans. Some have
been illegal. Some have been wicked, bad, nasty, crude, rude,
lewd, socially unacceptable, coarse, common and cheap. But
we've thought about them. "I wonder if I *could* get away with
that?" I've queried.

"No way," says the conscious (after due evaluation),
"She'd rip your lips off."

Joking aside, we have all received unworkable plans
from our subconscious minds, which have been momentarily
entertained and then discarded by the conscious mind. (Thank
goodness, or this whole society would be awaiting arraignment.)

Clearly, not every flash that comes from the subconscious is worthy of implementation. The conscious mind, with its dominant value system, must make those calls. Behavior does not ensue until the plans have been referred back to the conscious mind.

The conscious mind is ultimately responsible for interfacing any idea into the real world. Concepts of right and wrong, social mores, standards, and customs are issues that need to be dealt with in order for civilization to exist and survive. This, again, is the domain of the conscious mind.

(Hear it, Sigmund.) The subconscious cannot implement plans in the absence of conscious permission. Now this authorization *can* be subtle, and we are more susceptible to self-deception than many of us realize, but there is no behavior which lies outside the purview of the conscious mind! The subconscious mind cannot make you behave against your will.

In terms of creative capacity, we should see this yin-yang relationship between the conscious and subconscious as a marvelous advantage. You have one sector which can create and innovate without restraint or restriction. And you have another sector with the capacity to judge and override any inappropriate, unworkable or anti-social plans.

Your subconscious, the innovator, is not hampered by any given set of standards or norms. It deals with no barriers or fences when it comes to creating or problem-solving or inventing. The subconscious is free and uninhibited. It can turn things upside down, look at them from any and all angles of view whether they are "realistic," "possible," "workable," or not. It is free to pose, suppose and surmise. It has the unfettered freedom to postulate and innovate.

The subconscious mind is at total liberty to mull, consider, suppose, concoct, hypothesize, dream, devise, design, confabulate and form conjectures. It can create the impossible because it is not weighed down or restrained by any preconceptions, assumptions or mis-assumptions about what is possible. Breakthroughs which totally contradict "conventional wisdom" can be attained because the subconscious does not deal with right or wrong, workable or unworkable, practical or impractical. Oblivious to such values, it provides a limitless innovative capability.

Yet, there is a certain concreteness to the external world. We all have to live together on this planet, and so an override for the free-wheeling capacity of the subconscious mind must exist. The conscious mind passes judgment, retaining the power to veto or enact all plans, thus controlling behavior. In the final analysis, the conscious mind decides what goes and what doesn't.

Overall, this is generally a good thing, but it does have its down side. Even stunning, ingenious ideas can be summarily rejected at the whim of the capricious conscious mind. No bells, sirens or buzzers go off when the conscious mind rejects a million-dollar idea. The genius of the subconscious can be squelched in an instant by a hyper-judgmental conscious mind. Undoubtedly, billions of great ideas have gone down the drain, because of a closed, unappreciative or overly-critical conscious mind.

GIVING OURSELVES CREDIT FOR GENIUS

The evaluations of your conscious mind are voluntary and subjective. You pass the verdicts and make the value judgments. What criteria does your conscious mind use to formulate these crucial judgment calls?

Multiple elements affect the assessments. Values play a role. So do beliefs. So does culture. Education. Societal norms. All these form part of the frame of reference. Perceptions, habits, disposition and assumptions are heavily influential. Attitude is a factor. So is emotional state. Everything we have acquired over the years, and even transient factors such as our mood at the moment, enter into the equation.

When it gets right down to it, your judgment calls can be *very* arbitrary. Some days you are more critical than others, both of yourself and of others.

One of the things I hope you'll derive from this chapter is a respect for your own creative capacity. Sensitize yourself to your tendency to judge and dismiss your own ideas too quickly. If you will be more "open-minded" with your subconscious flashes, you may astound yourself with how much value your mind can produce.

Recently, in one of my corporate seminars, an engineer cited one of his co-workers for whom he held immense respect. His colleague had achieved numerous patents for his company. This was this innovator's trademark:

> Whenever I have one of these "wild ideas" leap into my mind, *I check it out right away.* Some of them don't work out, but a lot of them do.

I want you to start doing the same. Don't be so harsh on your own creative genius. When you have an idea bolt onto center stage, give it a chance. Consider it awhile. "Check it out right away."

SUDDEN BOLTS

Have you noticed the verbs and adverbs we have been using? Bolt, flash, leap, burst, suddenly, unexpectedly? Leonardo Da Vinci talked about ideas that would come to him in this manner. He called them, "fiamine della mente." (Italian for, "lightnings of the mind.") He said:

> The ideas that would *suddenly* come to my awareness proved to be most worthy and were in the end found to be infallible in leading me to discoveries of great importance.

Thomas Paine recognized the value of these flashes and considered them of utmost importance.   In 18th century language, he penned this description:

> Any person, who has made observations on the state of progress of the human mind, cannot but have observed that there are two distinct classes of what are called thoughts: Those that we produce in ourselves by reflection and the act of thinking, [*what I am calling conscious mind activity*] and those that bolt [*very interesting verb*] into the mind of their own accord. I have always made it a rule to treat these voluntary visitors with civility, taking care to examine, as well as I was able, if they were worth entertaining; and it is from them I have acquired almost all the knowledge that I have.

Paine taught himself not to be hasty, to examine those "sudden" ideas carefully. If you are going to do "business better than usual," you must do likewise. Teach yourself to restrain judgment a bit more. Allow yourself to stretch the limits of what you think may be possible. Don't be so quick to stamp the "that's not realistic" label on your strokes of genius.

Geniuses allowed themselves to consider the implausible, the impractical. By entertaining such ideas and letting the conscious mind and subconscious work together, they took the initial concept and produced a dramatic new outcome.

CAPTURING THE FLASHES

Since geniuses get their ideas the same way as the paper boy down the street, the difference may simply lie in what they do with those ideas. Geniuses may just be unique in that (1) they respect those thoughts, and (2) they capture them.

Have you had the frustrating experience of receiving a wonderful idea, becoming momentarily distracted, and then, not for the life of you, been able to re-conjure it? (It's one of the most excruciating experiences of life.)

Such experiences tell us that the subconscious mind is not terribly persistent. It never says to the conscious mind, "Whoa; I've been laboring long and hard on that idea. That was a great dominant thought you gave me a while back; and I've been spending weeks working on that one. If you aren't impressed, I am, and I'm going to put it to work anyway without your permission."

That never happens. The subconscious mind flashes the idea once, maybe twice. If the conscious mind vetoes the idea or just ignores it, that is the end of it. If you do not pick up on it, the subconscious doesn't seem to care. Dutifully, it goes off to work on another idea.

Flashes of inspiration last only a second, and then they're gone. Capture those fleeting insights. Record them in your organizer. (Here again is a prime reason for using only one system and keeping it with you.) While a napkin or envelope may suffice in a pinch, these scraps are as easily lost as the idea itself.

Since these flashes come when your conscious mind relaxes, you need your organizer with you wherever you go. Even at night, keep it nearby to record the thoughts that come spontaneously during those hours.

Frequently, you will find that when you *do* write down the first thought, another will flow in, right behind it. As you record that idea, another comes, and then another. It all goes back to "Mind thinks exclusively." Even thoughts from your subconscious come sequentially, like train cars on a track. When you take one off the track, the next one can take its place.

FROM FLASH TO FACT

When the subconscious flashes a plan to the conscious mind, three things can happen. The conscious mind can (1) ignore the idea, or (2) it can reject the idea. If the conscious mind ignores or rejects the idea, that's the end of the sequence.

However, one other thing can happen. The conscious mind can (3) accept the idea. When that occurs, the subconscious mind gets involved one more time.

- 4 -

THE SUBCONSCIOUS MIND IS THE PORTAL TO THE BODY

The subconscious mind executes the physical creation. Every move you make, every breath you take (call "The Police," what a lyric), everything—from basic body operation to complex coordinated movements—is managed by the subconscious mind. Like crews on ships, the subconscious keeps the "engine running," all systems functioning, ready and waiting for specific commands from the conscious to put the body in gear.

The conscious mind does not control the body directly. Its conduit to the body passes through the subconscious mind. If you want to pick up a pen to make a note in this book, you do not, with your conscious mind, command all the myo-neural synapses in your body. The conscious mind merely says, "Pick up the pen," and subconscious mind governs the intricate commands guiding the body to successful completion of the task or performance.

Take that concept now to a higher plane. Apply it to goal achievement, for example. It works identically. The conscious mind selects the target, and the subconscious mind will direct the body, quite accurately, to hit even the loftiest target.

THE FOUR-STEP SEQUENCE

To summarize, let us rehearse the sequence:

(1) Conscious Mind Activates Subconscious Mind With Dominant Thought.

(2) Subconscious Mind Develops Plans To Realize Dominant Thought, and Flashes Them To The Conscious Mind For Evaluation.

(3) Conscious Mind Evaluates And Approves The Plan.

(4) Subconscious Mind Governs Body To Bring The Plan Into Working Reality.

This marvelous interdependent relationship goes on all the time, forming, shaping and governing human behavior and performance.

CHAPTER 20

Pictures in the Subconscious

Mary Lou Retton, Olympic gold medalist in gymnastics, dreamed—and marveled at the outcome:

> I come from a very small coal-mining town in northern West Virginia. Who would have ever thought that I would become an Olympic champion? Not me, and my chances weren't very great. But I had a dream...and it did come true...it was something inside of me that said, 'Gosh, maybe I can make it to the Olympics someday.' And just that small little quote kept me going and made me work out every day in the gym rather than being with friends at the mall hanging out.

Priscilla Welch, Marathon champion, dreamed—and marveled at the outcome:

> [After winning the New York City Marathon, she said:] It sort of frightens me even today; it's surprising what you put in your mind if you really want something. You put that goal deep into your subconscious, and when you actually get it, it's a little bit scary.

I want you to dream, too, and marvel at your outcomes. To understand why dreams work so powerfully, how they produce results and, most importantly, how to put it all to work for you, three more insights about your subconscious mind are needed.

First, we know that the subconscious is, or has access to, **a vast repository of data**. Every page you have ever read, every lecture you have ever attended, every experience, every conversation, is recorded in the subconscious memory banks.

That does not mean that we always have ready access to that data. Most of us, at one time or another, have been frustrated with our conscious memory. In my classes I teach: Whatever is not repeated at regular intervals to the conscious mind will be lost.

When we were young, we memorized lengthy poems or works like the Gettysburg Address. Because these have not been repeated over the years, our memories have faded, and the verbatim precision has vanished in the gray matter.

But, take heart, to your subconscious mind, nothing is ever lost. You are a walking library of billions and billions of bits of data. You have collected immense amounts of information via your five senses. Studies indicate, even "background" input enters your subconscious data banks. While you carry on a conversation, a radio or television can be playing in the background. Although you may not be consciously focused on the broadcast, your subconscious mind picks it up. In effect, you know thousands of things that you don't even know that you know.

This tremendous repository is available in the creative process. In consonance with conscious thought, the subconscious mind searches the library, correlating data. Somehow, through ways which are still unknown, the subconscious organizes information, putting the data together, deducing plans.

THE POWER OF PICTURES

The second thing we know: The subconscious works primarily in **pictures, not in paragraphs.** That is, in fact, one of the grand distinctions between the two sectors of the mind. The dominant language of your subconscious is pictorial. It works in images. By contrast, the dominant language of the conscious mind is linguistic. It works primarily in words.

Right now, in your conscious mind, you are thinking in English, conversing with yourself in English paragraphs. If you have ever learned a foreign language, you know there comes a time when you actually start thinking in that other language, and that's when you really own it. At that time, the sequence of your words changes. Though the concepts may be essentially the same, the order of your thoughts is dictated by the language.

Words are the main medium of conscious thought. In contrast, the primary language of the subconscious is imagery. You can validate this from your own experience. When ideas flash into your conscious awareness from the subconscious, instantly you have a panoramic vision. The insight is conceptual or pictorial, not verbal. When you try to explain what you see to someone else, it takes several minutes to convert it into vocabulary. You struggle to put it into words. You *see* it, you understand it, but you have a hard time putting it into speech.

This correlates with what educators know about mental development and teaching young children. In preschool and kindergarten, the best way to teach a child is through pictures, demonstrations and experience. Lectures don't work as well. When you lecture to a three-year-old, you're not "speaking their language." Their cerebral cortex has not yet developed sufficiently to facilitate linguistic learning. Show them, they get it. Lecture to them, they don't. They hear the words, but they cannot easily convert them into comprehension.

PICTURES NOT PARAGRAPHS

Now, which language proves more influential when it comes to behavior? The portal to the body is the subconscious; the primary language of the subconscious is pictures. Pictures propel physical performance.

In athletics or dance, conscious paragraphs actually impede performance. When you are talking to yourself, saying, "I've got to turn here, shift my weight, pivot," etc., you are not at your best. Instead, when you are immersed in the event, absorbed in the moment (and your conscious mind stops babbling), you perform at optimum levels, physically and aesthetically. In those instances, your conscious mind almost becomes a spectator. With permission, the subconscious acts as implementor, moving you in synchrony with the rhythm and activities around you.

Thus, in many ways, you are already aware of this grand distinction between your two minds: The conscious mind works primarily in words; the subconscious works primarily in pictures.

This fact should save you a lot of money on the golf course. Golf is cruel; it forces you to take responsibility for yourself. I played baseball right on through college, and shortstop was my preferred position. In baseball, there was always a way to excuse lousy performances. You know, "Ball hit a rock;" "Sun got in my eyes;" "That was a bad call, Ump;" that kind of stuff.

In golf, the ball just sits there. You're the only one with a club. If that ball does not go precisely where you want it to go, no one else can be blamed. That's a cruel game.

A friend of mine, an excellent golfer, has played the game enough that he has a lot of refined pictures in his mind. He belongs to a club and loves to take me golfing there. Our main objective is relaxation and friendship, but we do keep score.

Generally the day follows a predictable pattern. He usually gets well ahead of me on the early holes. Behaving fairly casually at first, in his conscious mind he concentrates more on conversation than golf. While telling me how his family's doing, how the business is going, he walks up to the tee. He doesn't take many practice swings. He just pulls his driver back and ("CRACK") drives the ball 280 yards straight down the fairway. Then he goes right back to his discourses. By the time we complete the fourth hole, he's usually well ahead of me.

On the fifth hole, I get even. This hole has a finger of a lake that crosses the fairway about 150 yards off the tee. The hazard is only about 80 or 100 yards wide. Under normal circumstances, a 275-yard drive would go well over that water. But I know mind management.

As my friend walks up to the tee, I say to him, "I don't even want you to think about that lake." (It's dirty pool isn't it? Actually it's dirty golf, and it works.) He now does what any red-blooded human being would do. He starts talking to himself. (The subconscious mind, which has been doing quite well without a lot of conscious-mind coaching, now gets bombarded with "frontal lobe driving.")

Paragraphs proliferate in his mind. "Dennis is right," he *says* to himself. "If there's one thing I'm not going to do today, I'm not going to hit the ball into the lake. It's only out there about 150 yards. It's right there in the middle of the fairway, but if there's one thing I'm not going to do, I'm not going to hit into the...."

The next sound you hear is, "Kerplunck." The sound you hear after that, you shouldn't repeat. He looks back with disgust on his face, and says, "I knew I was going to do that." (Precisely.)

Now, what just happened there? The message seems to be right: "I'm not going to hit it into the lake." But the "I'm not, I'm not, I'm not" forms part of a *paragraph*. The *picture* is "ball in lake." The subconscious, the portal to the body, guides the process in harmony and obedience to the *picture*. Thus, the ball does not pass "Go," does not collect $200; it collects moisture.

HABIT TRAPS

This explains why we have such trouble with diets and New Years' resolutions. Does this sound familiar? "I'm not going to eat that food. I'm going on this diet. My willpower will be iron-clad; I'm going to stay on this diet until I get to my perfect weight. I will *NOT* eat that food!"

What is the central image? Yep, food. (Actually, it's more like FOOOOOD. We are talking about basic human need here.) Food! The subconscious may actually start reasoning with the conscious mind, saying, "Excuse me, if we don't eat something, we're *both* going to die." Conscious mind responds, "You're right. Let's eat."

The next thing you know you're on a binge through the cupboards. Not a Ho-Ho, Ding-Dong, or Twinkie remains unscathed in the entire house. By noon on the first day of the diet, you have devoured every Dorito in the neighborhood. You are not only filled with carbohydrates and fat grams, you are filled with self-recriminations. "Why am I so weak?" you groan, "Why can't I do the things I make up my mind to do?"

The answer is, you're not making up your *whole* mind. You are trying to steer behavior exclusively with words. Remember, it's the image, not the words that drives body. One of the major pitfalls—what I call the "Habit-Trap,"—is **focusing on what you *don't* want to do**. It doesn't matter how many phrases—how many "I don't want to's" or "I'm not going to's,"—you put in front of an image, you still reinforce the image. You tend to bolster the very behavior you want to abandon.

A GIANT PROBLEM

During a break in one of my seminars, I was adjusting my projector when, strangely, the room seemed to get dark. I turned around to find myself in the shadow of a huge human being. I hadn't realized how large he was when he was sitting in the audience. When he unfolded himself, he was close to seven-feet tall. He was extremely well built, and at this time very animated. He said, "I want to see you in the hallway."

My immediate thought was, "Why didn't I take that karate class?"

In the corridor a few moments later, we met. Large as he was, he had my full attention. He began to speak, and as he did, he welled up with tears. "I started with this company on the ground floor," he explained. "I only have a high school education, but I've been conscientious. Gradually I've worked my way up the ranks. Now I'm the head of a department. I have to stand in front of people, and I have to communicate." As he was recounting this background, interspersed about every other word (I've cleaned this up a lot) was a profanity. He had a very coarse vocabulary. "But," he continued, "I have this one &*%#@ problem when it comes to speaking."

I said, "Let me guess."

"Yes, I know I have a foul mouth," he admitted. "That's what I've come to talk to you about," he said, "I can't tell you how *&%^&@ hard I've tried *not to swear.*"

"Ah, my friend," I said, "that's the Habit Trap. You keep trying *not* to swear."

"What do I do about that?" he asked.

"Here's a suggestion," I said, "Work on adding to your vocabulary, instead of subtracting."

I proceeded to outline a plan. Once a week he was to find a dictionary, pick out five or six vocabulary words, jot them down on a three-by-five card, and then keep the card with him. Four or five times *a day*, not once a week, not once a quarter, but four or five times a day, he was to look at the card. (See what I was striving for?—Dominant thought.) I asked him to read the words, close his eyes, and picture himself using those words with his peers and associates.

"But what do I do about the swearing?" he questioned.

"We'll come back to that later," I replied. Actually I knew we would not come back to the swearing at all. He would overcome his problem *by neglect*.

About 18 or 19 months later, he called me. He said, "Dennis, a miracle has happened."

I asked, "What?"

He said, "Not only am I developing a fairly rich vocabulary, I've almost completely quit swearing."

Why did that work? He created an image of a new behavior and repeated it with sufficient regularity the subconscious mind relinquished any other images about speech and accepted the new one. The new active image became dominant and therefore was sanctioned as the template for behavior.

If the subconscious could not relinquish old images and accept new ones selected by the conscious, you and I would never have any hope whatsoever of improving our behavior. We would be locked into the original images forever and would never be able to change. The first picture would prevail, permanently.

Gladly, the conscious mind *can construct* and *present* a new desired result any time. When a new picture becomes dominant, the subconscious aligns with it. This fact gives all of us a prompt, even immediate, means of improving our behavior.

You don't have to go back and dump all of your old baggage. You simply have to start thinking preferable dominant thoughts. (I was going to slam old Sigmund again, but you're probably getting tired of it.) The moment the dominant thoughts change, the subconscious dutifully responds. It never nostalgically hangs on to the past. It deals with your current, active images.

Of course, if you make the choice of rehashing old images, your subconscious will respond accordingly and will continue to produce what the "rehashed images" beget.

When it comes to changing human behavior, **HABITS ARE NOT BROKEN, THEY ARE REPLACED!** They're replaced with a new image—the current dominant image in your conscious mind—which redirects the subconscious.

SENSORY-RICH, EMOTION-LADEN IMAGES

The third thing we know about the subconscious is by far the most exciting. We not only know the potency of pictures, but we also know that nothing affects the subconscious and, therefore, ultimately our behavior, like **sensory rich, emotion-laden images**. The more sensory-rich and emotion-laden the images, the more powerful they are to the subconscious, the more quickly they are absorbed; and the more readily they are acted upon.

The advertising industry knows this and has turned its application into a fine art. Advertisers can take virtually any product, couch it in sensory-rich images and market it with great success. The first law of advertising, "Sell the sizzle not the steak," works.

Seldom are you shown the mechanics of a product. Instead, you are bombarded with sensory-rich, emotion-laden benefits—the perks which come from owning or utilizing the product.

McDonald's has done this marvelously well for decades. The folks at McDonald's do not sell you hamburgers, but they do a great job at selling you sizzle. If they were trying to sell you a hamburger point blank, occasionally in their commercials they would show one. (Have you ever noticed how little time they actually spend showing the food?)

We see deliriously happy people bursting into the restaurant with beaming smiles on their faces. They do pirouettes on the tables, and some even slide on their knees up to the counter to order something where the "hot stays hot" and the "cold stays cold."

Sitting out in television-land we marvel to ourselves, "I wonder if I could ever be that happy?" Over a hamburger?! It's not a very romantic product when you get right down to it. Just dead cow meat fried into a Frisbee shape.

We laugh, but we know how well it works. One time I was driving down the street with my toddler in the car seat. This child did not yet have a vocabulary that exceeded 12 words. But as we drove past the "golden arches," he lit up like he'd seen an angel descend from heaven, and he said, "Donald's!" He knew "mama," "dada," and "Donald's"?! (I don't care what you say, there's something wrong in a society, when the third word in a child's vocabulary is a trade name.)

Little people are not the only ones affected by this sensory-rich imaging. A case in point comes from the anecdotal history of the perfume industry. In the 1950s, one of the top-selling women's perfumes was Chanel No. 5.

Somebody had not quite caught on. "Chanel" was okay. Chanel has French overtones to it, and that's pretty good. (We all know what the French are famous for.) But "Number 5"?! Does that do anything for you? Close your eyes for a minute. Any real sensual images come to your mind when you contemplate the number five? Does it get you breathing heavy? Doesn't seem to do much for me.

Another perfume producer set a trend. A new perfume had been developed. What should the name be? A brain-storming session was held. Names were kicked around. Someone threw out a name and intended it to be funny. People in the room did laugh, but then someone else said, "Whoa, let's try it. Let's test market a perfume with that name, and let's just see what it does."

The perfume with the funny name became a best seller: "My Sin." Close your eyes for a minute. What images come to your mind when you picture "My Sin?" I rest my case.

"My Sin" started a trend that carries on today. Sensually provocative titles for perfumes are the rule. We have "Obsession." We have "Passion." They don't even leave us there, do they? The full name is "Passion by *Elizabeth Taylor*." (This isn't "Passion by Pee Wee Herman," it's "Passion by Elizabeth Taylor.")

Not long ago, walking through a classy department store, I saw the stuff I want my wife to wear—"Ambush!"

SENSORY-RICH VS. SENSUAL

Please note, sensory-rich does not necessarily mean sensual. That's the way Madison Avenue has it translated, but my use of the term sensory-rich is not so restrictive. Sensory-richness refers to the five senses of the body—hearing, taste, touch, smell, and sight. When images are saturated with sensory detail, the effect on the subconscious is immediate and remarkable.

Again, the subconscious mind is the portal to the body. The subconscious mind and the body operate in direct communication with each other. That which affects one, affects the other.

The senses of the body are potent communicators to the subconscious. Images saturated in sensory detail are quickly absorbed. Thoughts imbued with emotion act as stimulants, exerting instantaneous impact on the physiology. The satisfying experiences of sexual intimacy are obvious examples.

APPLICATIONS

Valid applications of this insight are virtually endless. Successful sales people use this concept to enhance the effectiveness of their presentations. They understand that people make purchases based on emotion, not logic. (Oh, people may try to justify their purchases with logic, but the bottom line is passion.)

Several car dealerships have set records using our technology. Their sales people learn to emphasize the sensory-rich aspects of their cars. Descriptions of smells, colors and textures, as well as convenience and luxury features, reach the buyer on a subconscious level. Emotion generates action.

"Imagine, Mrs. Jones, the advantages of fine Corinthian leather. It never gets hot in the summer, the way vinyl does. Leather always feels good on your skin, smells good and is so easy to maintain. The interior of your car will appear new and beautiful even after months of heavy back-seat use."

"Just picture yourself, Mr. Smith, driving down the road on a warm, spring day with the sun-roof open, the fresh air wafting in. And, with the features this model offers, you'll know what real driving pleasure can be like."

Well, you get the picture, don't you? Despite my facetious descriptions above, I hope you grasp my dead-serious point: Sensory images sink deep, and they incite action.

Master teachers also sense this principle. Telling stories, painting detailed verbal portraits, they create mental pictures in the minds of their students. Similarly, students who can translate the words of dry lectures into lush images learn faster. What's more, the learning endures and becomes far more accessible, even to the conscious memory.

High achievers in all fields use this principle either intuitively or cognitively. They see, feel, smell, and taste what they want. There really is something to the adage, "I wanted it so badly, I could taste it."

THE VISION OF VISIONEERING

Now you can see why I define visioneering as the engineering of dreams into reality **through sensory-rich mental imaging.** Vision is the element which integrates all of your faculties. When you visualize your goals in sensory-rich, emotion-laden images, you combine conscious mind, subconscious, and the energy and passions of the body into one unified force. The melding of all your faculties vaults you to the highest attainable levels of human performance.

CHAPTER 21

The Prevalence of Visioneering

Vision opens the door to continuous improvement, or it slams it shut and locks it tight. The power of vision is total. It unites every other human faculty and brings them all to bear, directly and exclusively, upon the chosen subject or image. You see it before you say it, you see it before you do it.

As timeless as mankind, this concept has been grasped and communicated throughout the annals of human progress. Aristotle, 350 B.C., declared:

> The reasoning mind thinks its ideas in the form of images; and as the mind determines the objects it should pursue or avoid in terms of these images, even in the absence of sensation, it is stimulated to action when occupied with them.

Not what you see with your physical eyes, but what you create in your mind's eye determines your creed, your conduct and your character. These visions are the greatest determinants in what happens around you, to you, for you and because of you. Your very circumstances and what you experience in life amount to the vision you have projected into the world.

Images organize and orchestrate action. No human act ever occurs without a mental blueprint. A boyhood mentor of mine, Sterling W. Sill, said:

> ...this picturing power of the mind is the greatest gift that
> God has ever given to man. It has the ability to construct
> images of success before the actual experiences are born. It
> can paint pictures that will fire our wills and exalt our
> spirits. This ability to travel ahead of our own success can
> also set up some giant, magnetic attractions at the very end
> of the trail that will draw us on with the greatest pleasure
> towards the most worthwhile objectives.

That we may create our own blueprints, and do so at will,
is at once both exhilarating and sobering. This faculty works
equally well, just as potently, in two directions—for better or for
worse, for richer or for poorer, for sickness or for health. (And,
in this case, from this potentiality, not even in death do we part.)

Two forms of visioneering exist: CONSTRUCTIVE and
DESTRUCTIVE. One of these two creative forces is always at
work. They cannot function simultaneously. Since mind must
think or, in other words, mind must create, every waking moment
you are building up or tearing down. Mental creation is constant
and incessant. You and I cannot evade the visioneering process,
but we get to choose how to employ it.

IT HAPPENS ALL THE TIME

Once, in one of my Power Goaling seminars, a man
expressed a concern:

> I've been at this point before. I know what will happen; it
> happens to me all the time. I'm going to get all revved up
> about a new goal and walk into my boss' office. She'll give
> me a couple of minutes to explain my idea, then she'll shoot
> it down, tell me to get back and do my job. That will be the
> end of it all. I'll walk out of her office feeling down, worse
> off than when I walked in. My plans won't go anywhere,
> and my boss will think I'm a do-nothing dreamer. I'll be
> better off if I just stick to the routine and forget this stuff.

Do you see what he just did? *He used visioneering to invalidate visioneering.* What he described was a mental movie, and it acted as a creative force. In this instance, he created rejection and defeat for himself. Obviously, to prove his point, all he would have had to do would be to act on his vision. Pursuing that blueprint, his precise vision would come to pass. The whole image would be enacted a few days hence in his boss' office. Following that experience—one that he alone had created—he would then declare that he had "evidence" to support his claim.

Obviously, he does not allow this episode to go to its negative conclusion. His track record of "actual events" so brims with "evidence," that he does not have to go that far. He saves face (and all that anguish) by just pulling the plug on the vision before he enacts it. "Only smart thing to do," he reasons, "No use putting myself through the pain and embarrassment."

By his own admission—"it happens to me all the time"—he has established a pattern but doesn't realize it. Ironically, he has learned the truth: **What he pictures in his mind is what really happens**. Unfortunately for him, he has focused his visioneering on the negative, limiting side of the coin. Every time he has envisioned rejection and defeat in the past, what he got was rejection and defeat. Never failed. Worked every time. No reason to believe it will be any different now or in the future. It hadn't occurred to him that the very same methods could be employed in a constructive way with the same, sure dependability.

Do you see it? He has developed, without realizing it, iron-clad faith in the principle of visioneering—negative visioneering. He does not see what an expert, accomplished visioneer he really is. He has become a perfect producer of destructive mental creation. He employs visioneering, with flawless consistency, on counterproductive visions.

He goes through life believing that his conviction is based on evidence, and it is. But, unfortunately, he does not see that all that evidence has been generated by his own self-ful-filling prophecy.

FAITH IS BASED ON EVIDENCE, YES!
BUT THE EVIDENCE IS SELF-CREATED!

Dr. Rod Gilbert wrote: "Losers visualize the penalties of failure. Winners visualize the rewards for success." Each of us reaps what he or she sows. The vision comes true.

We do not realize how strong we are. We are so potent in our visioneering that very few of our visions fail to happen. Each one we enact happens pretty much as we envision it. Some of the details may vary, but the essential vision takes place.

Every vision we create has an effect. No exceptions. Even those we don't enact still have consequences. Most of us are well conditioned visioneers, only we don't call it visioneering. We call it worrying. We call it "being realistic." We call it "being in touch with the real world."

We work out many visions meticulously in our minds, and then cancel them. We can see "where that one leads," and we shut down the process. We think because we don't enact them that they do no harm. But there are effects. Dwelling on negative thoughts leads to negative planning, which precludes the creation of positive, workable goals.

The man in the example above pictured what wouldn't work and ended it there. He thinks he was smart, that he beat the system. But he didn't "beat" the system, he misused it. He could have used his visioneering capacity (the same amount of time and mental effort) to devise ways of overcoming the opposition. If he was really commited to his goal, he could create the way to achieve it. ("Where there's a will, there's a way.") Knowing his boss as well as he did, he could have developed ways of enrolling her in his goal and could have moved that vision forward.

Even though he did not enact the negative plans, he still reaped a "harvest"—the harvest of squandered time and underemployed resources. It is not just a matter of what he didn't do that would have been bad, it is a matter of what he could have done that would have been good.

It is tragic how many hours some of us spend fretting over visions of what could go wrong. We spend precious time delving into the past, ruing and regretting, reliving again and again experiences which only reinflict the same pain and anguish. Worrying, fretting and regretting are forms of destructive visioneering.

What could we accomplish if we would cast out the negative, stop the counterproductive visioneering, exercise a little faith, and exclusively visioneer the positive?

THE GREAT SECRET

Can you picture Charles Barkley and Rush Limbaugh in the same room? That would be quite a duo. Well it happened. In 1993 Limbaugh had "Sir Charles" on his program. Barkley, the NBA's 1993 Most Valuable Player, expressed his views candidly and forthrightly on a variety of topics, including success and failure in life. At the end of the segment, after Barkley had left the room, Rush Limbaugh made this comment:

> I want to make one observation here, folks. I asked Sir Charles several times to describe the obstacles he's overcome. And he listened, and he heard me, but he did not do that. He didn't want to talk about what he's overcome. He just wants to concentrate on what he does best. I think it's important to point out that he didn't say: "Yeah, it was really tough for me. I had this and that." Here is a man **totally** focused on achievement. Which is why, my friends, he is dazzling the country with his prowess.

The thing that makes Barkley a champion, one of the best in his field, is not his body. One of the top rebounders, passers and scorers in the game of giants, he is barely 6'4". Most guards are taller than he, yet Barkley is the NBA's premier power

forward.   He achieves greatness by visioneering constructively—*only* constructively.

What he has done or been through in the past matters
little. Charles Barkley will not even run a short negative clip
from an old movie in response to a question. He focuses totally
and completely on what he wants to create *now.*

Dr. Frederick Green, a brilliant psychiatrist, who often
works with professional athletes, made an interesting observation. Several people were discussing Charles Barkley in a
casual setting. One person attributed Barkley's success to "great
passion and desire."

Dr. Green disagreed:

> Many athletes have as much desire as Charles Barkley.
> Many people in the NBA, and many who did not make it to
> the NBA, have as much or more desire than he. Barkley's
> success lies in his ability to focus on productive images. He
> focuses entirely on what he wants to have happen.
>   When most players whirl toward the basket, they see
> three defenders and try to figure out how to get past them.
> Barkley doesn't do that. He pictures himself scoring, and
> lets the three defenders figure out how they are going to try
> to stop him.

Consistent winners, like Charles Barkley, focus exclusively on constructive visioneering. They eradicate the flip-side
from their minds. They know the great secret: **Visioneering
works—and it works all the time, and it works every time.**

We reap, each time and every time, the exact fruits of our
dominant visions. Every victory in business or personal life;
every victory on the playing floors, fields, rinks, courts or
diamonds of sport; every victory in courts of law, or on floors of
legislatures; every victory, military or moral, is first fought and
won on the visionary screens of our minds! What we project
onto our screens is what we get in life. Truly, the mind is our
"ultimate arena of battle."

To achieve more consistent victories, we must:

(1) Recognize how much visioneering already works in our lives,

(2) Become more aware of when we misapply visioneering, and

(3) Amplify our constructive visioneering.

VIDEO CASSETTES

Visioneering is so much a part of us, it is virtually second nature. We do it so automatically, we seldom detect that we're doing it. In seminars I sometimes endeavor to point this out to the participants. Painting some mental pictures of everyday situations, I ask people to notice what thoughts come to their minds by habit. I call these habitual patterns of thought "video cassettes."

Many students begin to recognize some of the cassettes they pop into their "VCR player" in response to common episodes. When they analyze the scripts of their videos, they recognize how unproductive many of them are.

To illustrate, let me share one of my own "junk cassettes" of the past. (I often use this in seminars to help others recognize some of their own.) Whenever I would find myself in a less-than-ideal situation, I would plug in the "If-Only-I-Hadn't" cassette. If unhappy with my finances, for example, I'd visualize my past. "If only I hadn't bought that four-plex. If only I hadn't spent so much money on that car. If only I hadn't strayed from my budget..." The video would run on and on. After a few hours of "if-only-I-hadn't-ing," I could tell you precisely where I had fouled up, and exactly how I got to be in that fix. Then, over and over again, I would repeatedly lament those decisions. But how productive was all that lamentation? Bad cassette.

One day I realized that visioneering the errors of the past was not only unproductive, it was counterproductive. Cassettes drive behavior. Bad cassettes generate bad results. I'm not saying we shouldn't evaluate or learn from our mistakes. It's the frequency and repetition I'm deploring. We're not such slow learners that we have to replay the "If-Only-I-Hadn't" cassette as a daily feature.

A better cassette to play would be "Where-Do-I-Want-To-Go-From-Here?" Or, "What's-My-Best-Option-Now?" Or, "What-Advantages-Can-I-Create-Out-Of-My-Present-Situation?" Or any number of other more useful cassettes.

In my seminars, once I have illustrated the point, I have the participants take five or ten minutes to create constructive scripts to replace some of their own commonly played cassettes.

One day, a man in my class rolled his eyes, stared up at the ceiling with a "Someone-please-save-me" look. Something prompted me to approach him, and I said, "Sir, you don't appear to have much value for this exercise."

"That's right, I don't," he said.

"Care to share with the rest of the class why not?"

"What you are having us do isn't real. We're just making this stuff up," he said firmly.

The teaching opportunity could not have been more perfect. Every ear in the class was alert, waiting to hear my response.

"That is right," I said. "You are absolutely right. We are making every one of the new cassettes up. They are not real; they are entirely, utterly made up. AND SO ARE THE OLD ONES! The old, habitual cassettes are not *real* either. We made them up, too. The only difference is, we have replayed them so many times in our minds that they *appear real* to us. They seem to be reality. WE CREATE EVERY ONE OF OUR OWN CAS-SETTES. FOR GOOD OR FOR BAD, THEY ARE *ALL MADE UP!* The question becomes, which cassettes are productive?"

You could have heard the paint drying on the walls. It was one of the most electrifying teaching moments I have ever experienced. The man, and every other person in the room, *got it!*

We all understood at that one instant, how literally we produce and project our own cassettes. We all knew how precisely we create our own lives through those visual productions.

For each of us the most venerable accomplishment in life is the rooting out of the old videos and replacing them with better, more positive (IRONICALLY, MORE CORRECT) images. Visioneering is not only the principle, but also the method, whereby we accomplish this feat.

Aristotle re-echoes:

> The reasoning mind thinks its ideas in the form of images; and as the mind determines the objects it should pursue or avoid in terms of these images, even in the absence of sensation, it is stimulated to action when occupied with them.

What type of images do you want to have stimulating you to action? Recognize how much visioneering already works in your life. Become more aware of times when you may be misapplying the principle of visioneering, and follow me to the next chapter to learn how to amplify your constructive skills.

CHAPTER 22

The Visioneering Technique

Visioneering, defined as the engineering of dreams into reality through sensory-rich mental imaging, might seem a little daunting. Usually, when I describe visioneering as the running of mental movies until they are as believable as a memory, people become more comfortable with the term. When I relate a story about my son and visioneering they know exactly what I am talking about.

JARED AND THE FINAL THREE SECONDS

One Saturday morning I glanced out a window of my home to see my son, Jared, out on our basketball court (which occasionally serves as a driveway). He dribbled a basketball, seemingly all alone in the world. No brothers, no pals from the neighborhood participate. It's just Jared, the ball, the concrete court and the hoop.

If you will do a little visioneering yourself here, picture Jared with no other players around to join in. You may be picturing him bored. Possibly, you may be assuming, he longs for someone to show up so he can play a game. Such assumption would be inaccurate. Jared is anything but bored. He *is* playing a game. It happens to be one of the most exciting and crucial basketball games in the history of mankind.

Three seconds remain on the clock, my team trails by one point. But I have the ball...three, two...the seconds click down...I put my move on the man guarding me. With the final second showing on the clock, I jump high into the air, fire my jump shot.

(Jared shoots. The ball rims out. Does not go in.)

No, that wasn't it. Three seconds remain on the clock, my team trails by one point. But I have the ball...three, two...I put my move on the man...I jump high into the air, fire my jump shot.

(The ball goes in this time.)

It's Goooodd!

(Jared hurls triumphant fists into the air. With both hands raised, he parades around the driveway.)

and 22,000 screaming, adoring fans chant, "Jared, Jared, Jared...".

Do you remember when we used to do that as children? We rehearsed our victories, enacting segments of our future lives, in great, sensory detail. That's visioneering.

As I mentioned earlier, when we came into this world, we possessed a well-developed, sensory-imaginary capacity. Somewhere along the line we become inhibited about that ability. We think we must become all logic and analysis. While those aspects of mental ability are certainly worth cultivating, the visionary capacity and proclivity of our childhood should not be pushed aside. Visioneering is the great programming and triggering mechanism of the creative genius inside us. It's not child's play.

RECAPTURING AND REFINING THE TALENT

To enhance the positive effects of visioneering in our lives, we need to simply practice a bit. The skills, which may have temporarily gone dormant through disuse, can be reestablished.

> That which we persist in doing becomes easier to do; not that the nature of the task has changed, but that our capacity to do it has increased.

So observed Ralph Waldo Emerson, one of the most insightful figures of the previous century. The best way to refine your abilities and improve your constructive visioneering is to make it a formal exercise for awhile. Eventually, these more formal sessions will be replaced with spontaneous application, but you will benefit greatly by "getting back to the basics," and starting with a formal practice session.

Here's what I recommend:

STEP 1: MINIMIZE EXTERNAL DISTRACTIONS

For your formal sessions, find a calm, quiet location, someplace where you are unlikely to be disturbed. Find a place with few sensory distractions. If you are in a room that has blinds, trim the shades so you're not subject to a lot of external diversion. (Increased attention span, as recommended in Chapter 14, will be an additional asset here.)

Edison, when he was concentrating, seeking breakthroughs, would lock himself in what amounted to be an oversized closet. There were no windows or pictures on the wall. The room was sensorially deplete. The only furnishings were a table and chair and a light bulb (which he had invented on a previous session there) hanging down from the ceiling.

STEP 2: ELIMINATE INTERNAL DISTRACTIONS

Get comfortable. I recommend that you sit up. (If you lie down, the session will likely develop into a nap.) Close your eyes, and unwind. Don't try to guide your mind at first. Just relax.

Typically, your mind may initially wander, dealing with some menial matters, like: "I wonder if I turned the water off in the back yard," or "I wonder if the porch light is on." Dismiss such thoughts if you can. If something valuable crosses your mind, if you have an idea you wish to remember, get up for a moment and write it down.

Otherwise, stay seated; relax and unwind.

STEP 3: EMPLOY RELAXATION TECHNIQUES

Relaxation doesn't have to be complicated. Lengthy relaxation procedures are not necessary. A few simple elements work very well:

(1) Relax the muscles of your neck and upper back.

It may be more than coincidental that when we allow ourselves to become stressed, the muscles of our neck and upper back become tense, tight and contracted. The location of the tension strikes me as more than symbolic It seems almost as though some force tries to severe mind-body communication.

When the muscles of the neck and upper back become taut, blood flow from the heart to the head is impeded. As a result, thought, judgment and decision-making are adversely affected. In turn, constrictions in the neck hamper optimum flow of the secretions from the brain back to the body. Governing molecules are restricted and obstructed.

One of the best ways to relax the muscles of the neck and upper back is with an exercise called, Head Rolls. While seated, simply drop your chin to your chest. Rotate your head, slowly, in one direction around the axis of your neck. Allow gravity to do as much of the work as you can. Make a few rotations in one direction, then reverse, and do a few in the other direction. Pay attention to the muscles as you rotate. Concentrate on feeling the stretching of the neck muscles more than the movement of your head.

A second method of relaxing this area of your body is the Shoulder Shrug. Elevate your shoulders toward your ears as far as you can. (Be sure not to go above the top of your head. Just kidding.) Now rotate your shoulders backward, pulling your-shoulder blades together. As you rotate your shoulders backward, let your chest expand, and take a deep breath.

Those two simple techniques will relax you where you need it most.

(2) Focus on your breathing.

With your muscles relaxed, concentrate on your breathing. Don't try to control it, just become aware of it. Center your thoughts only on your breathing—the breathing out, the breathing in. Do this for about 30 seconds. As you focus on your breathing, become aware of how you are breathing.

When you are tense you tend to breath from your chest. The more relaxed you become, the more you do abdominal breathing. At first, don't alter your breathing, just become aware of it.

(3) Shift to slow, abdominal breathing.

As you center on your breathing, two things happen: First, you clear your mind of distractions and, second, you become more relaxed. After about 30 seconds of relaxation and centering, shift to deep abdominal breathing, and slow your rate down. Do this gradually, comfortably and naturally. Slowly and smoothly, let your diaphragm draw down into your abdomen. Your stomach will expand and contract accordingly. As you move to deep breathing, slow down. Take deep, slow, abdominal breaths.

(4) Let your cares go.

Set your cares and concerns aside. Unpack for a moment or two. Let things go. Take a totally passive attitude. Let go.

STEP 4: VISIONEER: RUN A POSITIVE MOVIE.

With your eyes closed, run your mental movie. Visioneer. Picture the pleasant experience, uplifting event or positive goal you desire. Make your movie as sensory-rich and as real as you possibly can. If any negative thoughts attempt to sneak onto center stage, dismiss them. Dwell on your dream, and savor all the positive feelings and emotions that will flow from realizing it.

Notice that visioneering sessions do not have to be lengthy experiences. Five minutes works wonders. In fact, when you get comfortable with the technique, you can close your eyes just about anywhere, relax a bit, and run your mental movie. In just a few seconds, you can renew yourself with this simple technique.

Once in a while (you don't have to do this every day, but you may want to) add some music to enhance the effect. Hollywood learned a long time ago about the effect of background music. Music can markedly enhance the emotional response to visual images without interfering with the vision itself. Well-crafted sound tracks can enhance the full gamut of emotions from tension to romance, heightening involvement and interest in the vision on the screen.

For such reasons, I advocate the use of music in your visioneering sessions. Ideal visioneering music is instrumental, no vocal to it. It should start out simply—melodically and softly—with only one instrument voice introducing the theme. As the theme develops, more instrument voices join in, the tempo accelerates, and the volume steadily crescendos. Such music produces an emotional effect which works well in conjunction with your visioneering.

Many movie titles and love themes fit this general description. Pick one that appeals to you. The decision has to be yours, and you need to select music which "floats your boat."

THE BENEFITS

It will take me several other books to even begin to catalogue and illustrate the myriad benefits and applications of visioneering. Yet, even a cursory summary, is impressive:

1. Increases mental strength

Were you to look at visioneering strictly as an exercise, it would have great merit for you. Your ability to concentrate will be enhanced by re-establishing your visualization ability. Your attention span will grow and will, in turn, amplify what you get out of your reading, your brain-storming and problem-solving sessions at work or at home.

By focusing your visioneering on a specific goal or object, you will soon recognize how good you really are when it comes to staying centered on one topic. If at first, you find your mind wandering, flitting to menial or mundane matters, persist. By holding a daily session at about the same time each day, you will notice, within two to three weeks, your ability to stay on topic will grow. Your mind will wander less, and you'll recognize gains in concentration ability and in lengthening your attention span.

2. Closes credibility gaps

Every successful person I have ever met, from Olympic champions to prosperous business people, have confided a certain amount of insecurity, self-doubt, and their share of fears. They have learned to overcome the crippling effects by focusing on their desired outcomes. Visioneering stands as the best weapon you can have in your arsenal for vanquishing fear, worry and doubt. These internal mutineers cannot survive the onslaught of sustained positive mental movies. Seeing yourself achieving your goal, solving your problems, being who you wish to be day in and day out, creates confidence and faith. Your vision of the future will prevail over those impostors of fear and doubt, and they will quail.

3. Triggers the creative-innovative centers of the subconscious

Vision begets vision. Visioneering sinks deeply into the subconscious mind. The subconscious, stimulated by the dominant thought of your visualized desires, searches memory banks, and develops plans to transform the vision into reality. Ingenious strategies and direct routes will flow into your mind to point the way to your desired destinations.

4. Creates a new state of being

Like seed, vision reproduces faithfully after its own kind. When your picture a better life—a higher state of being—natural and virtually automatic forces go to work to produce that better life and become that higher being. This principle provides the means of overcoming the "This Is Just The Way I Am" syndrome.

Visioneering, the pathway to continuous improvement, combines and ignites all your faculties and focuses them. Everything gears up to fulfill the visions in your mind's eye. Elevating what you "see" inside transforms your inner self, and your outer world must also change commensurately.

CHAPTER 23

Transforming Yourself

Phillips Brooks, theologian and philosopher, challenged us all to dream big in order to elevate our qualities:

> Pray not for tasks equal to your powers. Rather, pray for powers equal to your tasks. Then the doing of your work shall be no miracle—but *you* **shall be the miracle**.

Lifting your vision of your own capabilities, expecting more of yourself, seeing yourself as a more competent being, paves the way to continuous improvement.

Many high achievers have discovered that truth. They "see the future," they see the way they want to be, and view that unseen reality as though it were happening now. By this means, they organize and exert influence over those future events. Arnold Schwarzenegger used this precise technique (visioneering) to reach the pinnacles of two separate endeavors, as a body builder and movie star. He said:

> As long as the mind can envision the fact that you can do something, you can do it. I visualized myself being there—having achieved the goal already.

The ability to *"SEE and BE"* today, here and now, what you want to be; and to shape the future by, through, and with that vision, has been corroborated many times by experiences people have shared with me. One of the most gratifying and heart-warming of these examples is the story of Stuart E. Curtis.

After one of my seminars, he related this remarkable example of visioneering:

> I want to share an experience I had years ago. I did not call it visioneering, but I had a phenomenal experience as a young man which confirms everything we've talked about today.

He then went on to tell this story. Stuart Curtis grew up in the West, basically as a city boy, in a nice home on a city lot. A few of his friends, he thought, were more fortunate. They lived on ranches and rode horses. As they would recount their "cowboy" exploits, riding in cattle drives and "round-ups," Stuart longed to have such experiences too.

As a boy he did learn to ride a horse, but opportunities to perfect his skills were very few and far between. Yet his love for horsemanship never left him, and he attended every rodeo that came near his town.

For some reason, and to this day he still does not know why, he became totally smitten with the rodeo event called calf-roping. If you've seen a rodeo, you know how it works: A cowboy, poised on a trained mount, gets set and signals to a man at a chute. Crack, the chute opens, and out runs a panic-stricken calf heading at warp speed for the other end of the galaxy.

Like Roy Rogers on a good hair day, the cowboy, twirling the rope, rides at full tilt and overtakes the calf. Launching his lasso, the cowboy ropes the calf, bringing it to a rude and abrupt halt. Just as the calf regains its feet, the dismounted cowboy rushes to the calf, flips it onto its back, gathers three of the four feet together, and, finally, with what is called a "piggin' string," wraps and ties his prey securely.

Simple. Right?! Rrrightt. It takes even seasoned riders, who have grown up in a saddle, hours of repeated practice to develop the mind, body and horse coordination to master this event. Well, Stuart fell in love with calf-roping. He longed to become a calf-roping champion. His dream required a highly trained (thus rather expensive) rope horse with specialized tack and practice calves. As much as his parents wanted to provide Stuart with this opportunity, it just wasn't practical or feasible.

But the dream never dimmed. Stuart still had his heart set on becoming a calf-roping champion. One day, while browsing through "Western Horseman" magazine, he came across a book advertisement: *Calf Roping* by Toots Mansfield. It's not a best seller, but Toots Mansfield was an insightful guy. His book emphasized the need for consistent practice to keep the skills keen and well honed. "If you cannot practice with your horse every day," he wrote (I don't think Toots ever dreamed that you'd *never* get a chance to practice with your horse), "you still need to keep your roping skills sharp." He went on to suggest the making of a "target." "Out of scraps of lumber," he said, "make a silhouette, the size of a calf. Then, for 30 minutes each day, stand flat-footed and practice roping 'the calf' from different angles."

Stuart was absolutely delighted with Toots' suggestion. He gathered scraps of lumber and made a "calf." Out of his allowance, he saved enough money to start dressing the part. Every day after school, Stuart donned his rough-out boots, his cowboy-cut Wranglers (actually you have to put the jeans on first), his wide leather belt with gaudy belt buckle, and a plaid shirt with the pearl snap buttons. (If you're picturing him with a brown hat and a bandanna, that's optional.)

As a senior in high school, although he was nearly full-grown, Stuart was still playing cowboy in the front yard. He was nearly six feet tall with blue eyes and blond hair (for visioneering purposes, visualize a tall Robert Redford). And, he's totally dedicated to his dream. Every afternoon he practiced. He'd drag out his calf silhouette, take his trusty lasso and, in his mind, "rope and ride" with the best of them.

He ran this sensory-rich mental movie hundreds of times:

Mounted on my horse, I, Stuart E. Curtis, sit poised in the saddle, setting my boots firmly into the stirrups. A nervous calf waits, entrapped in a chute. A gatekeeper perches there, ready to release the calf at my signal. Twirling the lasso smoothly, pigging string between my teeth, a slight hush comes over the capacity crowd. Confidently, I nod to the gatekeeper. Out goes the calf! My horse and I, a synchronized team, lurch forward, streaking for the darting calf. We rapidly draw close to it, and...

(Stuart, faking a gallop, takes a few steps forward on his front lawn. He opens his eyes and there he sees his calf—that dumb wooden silhouette with no tail—and fires his rope.)

Got him! And the crowd roars approvingly!

Time and time again, Stuart Curtis lived his dream. "After a while," he said, "I got to be pretty good at the roping. I could lasso that 'calf' from almost any angle."

There's one part of the process which was missing, however. In the event, when you finally rope the calf, you have to throw it onto its back and with the pigging string secure three of the four legs. With a wooden silhouette, you can't do that. But Stuart had a German shorthair dog. (Are you getting ahead of me?) The dog's name was Fritz, and he was very obedient. Fritz would come when called. After practicing the roping skills, Stuart would call "Fritz." Fritz would come, and to Fritz's surprise, Stuart would grab him, throw him down on the lawn and secure Fritz's legs with the pigging string.

Fritz was fairly docile, but after five or six times of that every night even he wouldn't put up with it. So, Stuart would go back to roping the hunk of plywood.

Can you see the neighbors driving by? Can't you just see

them, saying out of the corner of their mouths, "Oh and he seems like such a nice boy too."? (Here he is, a senior in high school, playing cowboy every night, and assailing the family pet.)

Now, you need to know, in those days, in order to compete in the state high school calf-roping championships, you did not need to qualify. All you needed to do was send in an entry form. They'd take whoever applied and run them through the preliminary go-round. Paring the field down to the top ten, they would then run the final go-round, and then award the championship buckle.

Stuart said, "I didn't know if I'd ever get a horse, but I knew if I didn't send in that form I'd have no hope at all." Hoping on top of hope, he sent in his entry.

Shortly before the competition, Stuart made arrangements to borrow a trained rope horse from a friend who was also entered into the event. Yet even at that, there was no time to practice. The first time Stuart Curtis laid his eyes on that horse was the day of the state high school calf-roping championships.

And then, ladies and gentlemen, boys and girls, it came down to this: Only for the first time in his life was Stuart Curtis mounted on a real rope horse to rope a real calf. He said, "It wasn't that different from what I had pictured all those days in my front yard—except I was a lot higher off the ground." Mentally, he knew what to do. He went back to that familiar territory in his mind. In many respects, it seemed like he'd always been there.

Stuart got that lasso going, he looked over, and sure enough, there was a nervous calf in a chute and a gatekeeper awaited his signal. When Stuart felt ready, he nodded to the gatekeeper and out went the calf and out went Stuart Curtis after his dream.

He and the horse charged after that calf. He leaned over and heaved his lasso. There was a groan from the crowd. He had missed the head. But as fate (or whoever's in charge of rodeos) would have it, he had managed to rope one of the rear legs, and the effect was the same. Spoing! That calf came to a screeching halt. Instantly, Stuart hurled himself down off the horse. He grabbed the calf. ("You can't believe how much heavier it was than Fritz," he said.) He threw the calf onto its back, wrapped the pigging string three times around its legs, and Stuart's hands went into the air. When the dust settled, Stuart Curtis was in sixth place and going to the high school calf-roping championship round.

Now, only for the second time in his life, was Stuart Curtis mounted on a real horse to rope a real calf. (He said, "No sweat; this time, I'd had practice.") He put himself into his familiar mind set, nodded to the gatekeeper and out went the calf. Stuart's angle was perfect. He overtook the calf rapidly, threw his lasso right around the neck. A split second later he was down to the calf. Slam, the calf was on its back, the pigging string whipped around the legs, and Stuart's hands went into the air one more time. Clocks don't lie. Stuart Curtis was the fastest of them all that day—the 1962 Utah State High School Calf-roping Champion!

In the book, *Psycho-cybernetics*, Maxwell Maltz said:

> Your nervous system cannot tell the difference between an imagined experience and a "real" experience. In either case, it reacts automatically to information which you give it from your forebrain.

That statement underscores the power of vision. Visioneering gathers and combines all of your faculties, uniting them into optimum performance in every aspect of life. Apply this principle in whatever endeavor you choose, and the results will speak for themselves. As you visioneer loftier goals, more noble deeds, and stronger character, you continually transform yourself into an ever greater being.

CHAPTER 24

Empowering Yourself

"What do you want to *be* when you grow up?" We pose that question frequently to children, and tender it teasingly to one another as adults. It conveys a perspective that our ultimate ends are a state of being. I like that implication. It places emphasis (for a change) in the right place.

We live in such a materially-fixated society, it is somewhat surprising we don't ask, "What do you want to *have* when you grow up?" Gladly, we seldom hear that question.

Embedded in the question, "What do you want to be when you grow up?" lies yet another implication. We imply that our desired states of being must exist somewhere in the distant future. Who or what we want to be stands remote from us in the present. Not for the "Here and Now," we continually convey a sense of "Later on" and "Someday."

This subtle inference of "becoming" rather than "being" rests on the notion that, in order to "BE" something, we must "DO" some things. When we adopt this concept, we view "Being something" as a reward, as though what we *are* occurs as the result or consequence of what we have *done*.

This line of thinking leads to another assumption.   In order to *do* stuff, you must *have* some stuff.   You must be equipped and furnished and empowered with the necessary tools, supplies and resources to do and accomplish the steps that, in turn, enable you to be what you want to be.   The pitfall of this erroneous conclusion is bottomless.   HAVE → DO → BE never ends.

Take, for example, a newly organized business.   Often the principals will think something like this:

> Our goal is **to become** the number one company in our field.   That achievement will require that we **do** our job better than anybody else.   What we must **do** is work smarter and harder, make better products at lower costs, and get them out faster than the competition.   **To do** that we'll need **to have** several things: First we must **have** a Policies and Procedures Manual so everyone will know how to act and what to do when situations arise and...(And the list begins.   But it never ends.)

The leaders of this company will spend most of their time and energy on getting what they need to *have* in order to *do* what they need to do in order to *be* what they want to be.   HAVE must precede DO, which must precede BE.   They think.

Here is the trap: The HAVE list has no end.   Most lethally, from that point of view, the mind focuses on what we lack and why something cannot be done.   We form perceptions of destitution, deficiency and difficulty.   Bottom line, we create powerlessness.

CHOOSING EMPOWERMENT

Here's what I would recommend instead:

TAKE ON THE PERSONA OF YOUR VISION AND UNPACK.

Reverse the order of the traditional view, **HAVE → DO → BE.** Make it **BE → DO → HAVE.** Create a lofty, noble vision. Take on the persona of what your vision dictates, and watch what happens! The works and the fruits take care of themselves. You do and say the right things; and you will have, as a result of **who you *see* yourself being**, what you dreamed of and longed for.

When we follow this line of thinking, we liberate ourselves. We don't have to go anywhere. We can unpack and savor the moment and still accomplish great things. What we "want to be when we grow up" no longer stands so remote—some long-range reward, some destination we travel to, some goal we hope to attain someday. BEING happens *now,* if we will but create it.

When we focus on being, rather than becoming, everything moves forward into the present. Taking on the persona of our vision, brings all current resources—everything from personality to physiology—into alignment. We form perceptions of possibility, capability and confidence. Bottom line, we create empowerment.

RECREATING YOURSELF

Once you grasp the power in BE → DO → HAVE, and integrate that concept with the central theme of this book, you are ready, my friend, to discover fire. **Being is a creation!** We create it all—our personality, our moods, our character, our demeanor, our temperament, OUR STATE OF BEING—first mentally, then materially. To alter our thinking is to alter our being, and that alters every effect that flows thereafter.

The moment we alter our being—our "modus operandi" (our operating mode)—we simultaneously alter every subsequent effect.

Here's a personal example. In the past I have *been,* when I came home from work, Maintenance Manager. Without realizing it, that was how I was "seeing myself." Because that was my vision, I behaved like Maintenance Manager. The moment MM walked in the door his eyes spotted things out of order. Toys in the room. Books, shoes and backpacks strewn around. Dishwasher not emptied. Table not set. Maintenance Manager knew exactly what to do. He barked orders. "Pick up these toys. Whose books are these? Who left their socks in the family room? Jacob, empty the dishwasher. Timothy, set the table. Rachel, vacuum the carpet so we don't have to dine in all this squalor..." And Maintenance Manager got the job done.

There was (usually) no hand-to-hand combat to get the place shaped up, but neither was their much tranquility. The tone coming from Maintenance Manager was harsh, autocratic, dictatorial. Children obeyed, but something was obviously amiss.

Among several declarations of mine, one is: "I declare myself to be Loving Father." To take on that persona, I have visioneered many hours. I have pictured myself being a whole different personality than Maintenance Manager. When those sensory-rich visions run through my mind, they sink deep into the subconscious. After a little germination, new ideas—better modes of behavior—come flashing back into my conscious mind. I take on the persona of Loving Father.

Consequently, I do things differently as my days unfold. Things come out of my mouth, appear in my body language and show up in my behavior, which are consistent with Loving Father. The world shifts in my home.

When Loving Father walks in the door, the first thing he sees are children. (That, obviously, is inherently related to the definition of Father.) The children come first and foremost. Loving Father wants to know how things went today for his children. "What did you do in school?" "Let me see some of the work you brought home." "Anything fun, exciting or unusual happen?" LF hugs a few people. LF says, "Glad to see you; I kind of missed you these last few hours." Such statements are not contrived. They flow, naturally and spontaneously, out of the visual movie of how Loving Father acts.

Loving Father focuses on rapport. (MM on reports.) Rapport opens pathways for things to get done without the barking. "Jacob," LF would say, "would you mind emptying the dishwasher?" "Rachel, let's surprise Mom and have the table set, neat and tidy, when she walks in." LF gets the job done, too, but the environment and the outcomes are infinitely superior.

By their fruits, you shall know them. And the "fruits" show up *instantaneously*. The moment I take on Maintenance Manager, guess what fruits start showing up? I don't have to have anything. I don't have to wait for anything. The very instant I switch my visual movie to Loving Father, and thereby take on that persona, immediately those fruits appear. The effects flow, immediately, directly and rapidly from the cause.

When you see yourself being the person you desire to be, your mind opens up. Your confidence billows. Your creative genius ignites, and you see all sorts of ways of accomplishing your dream. What you need to do and say flow as a natural consequence. As circumstances arise and events unfold, you have a natural, flowing sense of "what to do" and "how to get it done." Take on the persona of what your vision dictates, and empowerment happens at that very moment.

THE CLASSIC EXAMPLE

One of the greatest examples of this principle shines out at the foundation of our nation. Thirteen scrubby colonies went up against the strongest military force on the face of the earth at the time. The sun never set on the British Empire. Imperial England had all the resources—human, monetary and military— to quell any rebellion.

Dispassionate third party observers would have seen an undertrained, ill-equipped, rag-tag, semi-organized coalition of frail states. The combined forces of farmers and field hands, of old and young, of fathers and sons, should have been no match for the mighty British.

But the revolution succeeded, despite the overwhelming odds, because the colonists *were not* "what was," they *were* "what would be." They won because they were more powerful than the British, and they were more powerful because they took on, right from the start, the persona of free people. They did not act out of their current circumstances (thirteen feeble colonies), they acted out of the vision of their desired results (a free and united nation). They were being free, not becoming free.

They sat down, and in written language, they declared themselves. They declared their state of being. They did not timorously say "Excuse us, King George, sorry to bother you, but, if you don't mind, we would really like to become...what we are hoping to be some day...what we are thinking of trying...what we want to have eventually...is our freedom."

No! Expressing and emoting their newly created state of being, something welling up forcefully from deep within their souls, they boldly declared:

> Know this here and now. We are free. Send over your red coats. Send over your ships. Bring your guns, your bayonets and your cannons. Nothing changes the fact, we are free!

Note their state of being:

> WE ARE. (Not a hope, not an aspiration, not a goal, but a *declared state of being.*) WE *ARE!* **WE ARE!** (Not future tense, not conditional.) **FREE!** (HERE. NOW. THIS INSTANT!) **FREE!** *WE ARE FREE!!*

The patriots' envisioned state of being was a source of tremendous empowerment. They took on their dream, completely and entirely. Their vision governed their plans, their words, and their conduct. They took on the persona of free people so strongly, great power—both internal and external— aligned with them and combined for their success. Their results ensued as morning follows midnight.

WRITE YOUR OWN
DECLARATIONS OF INDEPENDENCE

All that you accomplish, all that you affect, and all that you effect—all that you are—comes from the being you create and see and be, right now, in your thoughts. Create the desired vision. Take on the persona of your vision, unpack and experience the freedom and power that will furnish you.

Today, when you finish this book, sit down and write out some clear statements of who you declare yourself to be. Define your vision—your ideal—and take on that image through visioneering. Visioneer your declarations daily, perhaps when you first wake up and again at night as you retire.

Create your persona in sensory-rich detail. By doing so you will discover something. Those declarations will be **Declarations of Independence** for you, too. They bring you into the *present* tense. You can totally dispatch the mind-set of waiting: "Well, I'll sure be happy when I have...;" "I'll be so glad when I am...;" "Someday, hopefully and perhaps, when I have done enough, then I'll...."

Declare yourself to be "Loving Parent," for example, and take it on through visioneering. The fruits ensue immediately. You no longer have to be in a hurry to go somewhere because there is no place you have to *go!* Experience the joy of being present. Unpack. Live your dream. Now.

Look closely into the well known quotation from Henry David Thoreau. It has long been one of my favorites:

> I know of no more encouraging fact than the unquestionable ability of man to elevate his life by a conscious endeavor... If one advances confidently in the direction of his dreams, and **endeavors to live the life he has imagined**, he will meet with success unexpected in common hours.

Select a lofty vision, my friend. Visioneer yourself there, being, right now, the very person you desire to be, and watch how rapidly the empowerment occurs.

It is the consummate truth of life that you alter your destiny by altering your thoughts. The mind is your most crucial resource, your crowning asset, your ultimate arena of battle. If you will master the power of your mind, you may do or be whatsoever you will.

Index

Y

W

About the author:

Dennis R. Deaton is internationally known as a master teacher and corporate educator. He provides the tools and techniques for mastering the power of the human mind to thousands of individuals annually. His courses deal with every area of human development--including money management, stress management and goal achievement. But, they are all based on a single foundation--mind management.

Founder and Chairman of the Board of TimeMax, Inc., Deaton is the creator of the popular "Visioneering" technology, and producer of several audio cassette tape series, including "Visioneering™: The Art of Power Goaling." His book Money: An Owner's Manual is now in its third printing.

Deaton received his doctorate, cum laude, from Washington University. He and his wife, Susan, and their family live in Mesa, Arizona.

To learn more about Dr. Deaton's seminars or services, call TimeMax, (602) 545-8311.

Request for Information / Order Form

Please send free information regarding the following TimeMax products, seminars and/or services:

_____ **The TimeMax Organizer** - Day Planner

_____ **TimeMax live seminars**: Life Management, Visioneering: The Art of Power Goaling, Money: An Owner's Manual, Winning the Inner Game of Life (Total Mind/Body Fitness), and RelationSHIFT

_____ **Books and audio cassettes** by Dennis Deaton

_____ **YES!** **Add my name to the newsletter mailing list** so I may receive a **free** copy of *TimeLine*---filled with pointers for personal development, continuous improvement, and increased productivity---from TimeMax.

Name _____

Company's Name _____

Address _____

City _____ State _____ Zip _____

Daytime Phone _____Evening Phone _____

Book Order Form

Item	Qty	Price	Total
Money: An Owner's Manual		$11.95	
"The Money Owner's Kit" - (Instructions and forms for creating a comprehensive budget, savings and debt elimination plans)		$9.95	
The Book on Mind Management		$14.95	
The Book on Mind Management-hard cover		$29.95	
Tax (AZ add 6.5%)			
Shipping/Handling ($3.50 per book)			
TOTAL			

Telephone Orders: Call (602) 545-8311 - Have Visa, MC or AX handy.
Fax orders: (602) 545-8233
Postal orders: MMI Publishing, 1818 E. Southern, Mesa, AZ 85204

Manage your mind...about money!

Money: An Owner's Manual
by Dennis R. Deaton

Take personal money management to the MAX!
Meet--***and exceed***--your financial goals by learning to
create a new monetary mind-set:

> *"Clear thinking about money is what this book is
> about. When people get their bearings straight and
> think clearly about money, they become money wise.
> Being money wise, they avoid innumerable problems
> and wind up owning money---lots of it---instead of
> money owning them."*   - Dennis R. Deaton

Now in its 3rd Printing...*Money: An Owner's Manual*
is still just $11.95.
Order from TimeMax, by calling (602) 545-8311
or use the order form on the back of this page.

---

*"Money: An Owner's Manual is great. I'm reorganizing my financial life as
a result. Come to think of it, most of my life is being reorganized.
Checkpoint II is four months away. Wish I had this book 40 years ago!"*
    - Pat Campbell, E. I. DuPont

*"I read Money: An Owner's Manual carefully and put your ideas into
practice. Our income did not change, but we were able to pay off almost
$30,000 in debt, reducing our monthly payment by over $950. We have
acquired a financial freedom that we have never had before."*
    - Marta Klein

Request for Information / Order Form

Please send free information regarding the following TimeMax products, seminars and/or services:

_____**The TimeMax Organizer** - Day Planner

_____**TimeMax live seminars**: Life Management, Visioneering: The Art of Power Goaling, Money: An Owner's Manual, Winning the Inner Game of Life (Total Mind/Body Fitness), and RelationSHIFT

_____ **Books and audio cassettes** by Dennis Deaton

_____ **YES! Add my name to the newsletter mailing list** so I may receive a **free** copy of *TimeLine*---filled with pointers for personal development, continuous improvement, and increased productivity---from TimeMax.

Name _____

Company's Name _____

Address _____

City _____ State _____ Zip _____

Daytime Phone _____Evening Phone _____

Book Order Form

Item	Qty	Price	Total
Money: An Owner's Manual		$11.95	
"The Money Owner's Kit" - (Instructions and forms for creating a comprehensive budget, savings and debt elimination plans)		$9.95	
The Book on Mind Management		$14.95	
The Book on Mind Management-hard cover		$29.95	
Tax (AZ add 6.5%)			
Shipping/Handling ($3.50 per book)			
TOTAL			

Telephone Orders: Call (602) 545-8311 - Have Visa, MC or AX handy.
Fax orders: (602) 545-8233
Postal orders: MMI Publishing, 1818 E. Southern, Mesa, AZ 85204